About Art

About Art

Lisa Malcolm
Sally Dewar

S

Science Press

Front Cover:

Keith Haring. Untitled. 1982
Synthetic polymer paint on vinyl tarpaulin, 213 x 220 cm
J W Power Collection
Museum of Contemporary Art, Sydney

Science Press
Fitzroy and Chapel Streets
Marrickville NSW 2204
Australia
Tel: (02) 516 1122   Fax: (02) 550 1915

© Science Press 1989
A.C.N. 000 073 861

First published 1989

Reprinted 1990, 1991, 1992

National Library of Australia
Cataloguing-in-Publication data

Malcolm, Lisa.
  About art.

  Includes index.
  ISBN 0 85583 161 8.

  1. Art — Juvenile literature. 2. Art, Australian
  — Juvenile literature. I. Dewar. Sally. II. Title.

700

Set in Photos Roman and Futura Light
Printed in Singapore.

CONTENTS

Introduction

About Art has been designed for use by all secondary school students. Ideally *About Art* should be considered as a resource book for individual use enabling each student to work from it at their own pace, or it can be used by the teacher for programming art experiences.

The four parts of the book are designed to develop an understanding and appreciation of other artists' works and to encourage exploration of the students' world when seeking inspiration for their artwork. Information on specific skills has been provided, however, an emphasis on experimentation with media is encouraged. All the art activities can be used by students of different ages to develop works which are the students' personal responses to their world.

Students will gain an understanding and an appreciation of artworks by studying images and objects in Part I of the book. This section analyses the Elements and Principles of Design and how artists employ these through their various styles and techniques in making artworks.

Students can work individually through each chapter in class or as homework assignments. They are required to observe and respond to artworks both verbally and visually, through written responses and by making artworks.

Part II of the book can be used by both students and teachers. Teachers can use it as a source for the development of programs on a thematic basis for any age group for class or individual development. Students will find inspiration for experimentation with images and materials which lead to the development of minor and major works.

Part III is to be used in conjunction with Parts I and II as an explanation of techniques artists have used or students may wish to employ in making artworks.

PART 1
PRINCIPLES
OF DESIGN

Line

A **line** is a mark or a path, made by a tool or implement such as a pen, pencil, crayon, brush, or stick.

FERNAND LEGER, *Trapezists* 1954.
Oil on canvas, 390.6 x 371.6 cm. Collection: Australian National Gallery, Canberra.
©DACS 1988.

Questions

1 There is no perspective in this painting. What is meant by this statement?

2 What effect do the thick black outlines have on the representation of the two figures?

3 Have the bodies been simplified? If so, how?

4 What shapes in the rest of the painting relate to the two figure shapes? Why?

5 What effect do the different types of lines moving in different directions have on the overall mood of the painting?

Fernand Leger (1881-1955)

Trapezists is one of Leger's later works, depicting his love of the circus. In this composition figures are suspended from coils of rope and trapeze equipment. Thick black outlines are used to define volumes or forms of objects. Leger introduced this technique earlier in his career, during the 1940s.

Leger applied bands of brilliant colour across many of his paintings leaving it unrelated to the contours of his subjects. This style was called **painting outside the drawing.**

Leger was influenced by many artistic styles ranging from Cezanne's theories to Cubism, until he found his personal statement – 'strongly articulated forms in flat colour, outlined in black and animating the whole surface'.

FERNAND LEGER, *Divers on a Yellow Background* 1941.
Oil on canvas, 186.7 x 217.8 cm. Gift of Mr and Mrs Maurice E Culberg, 1953.176.

Line can be used to describe or **delineate** (outline) the **shape** or **volume** of the forms enclosed.

Combinations of lines can be used to represent **structure** and **movement** of forms.

PAUL KLEE, *Family Walk* 1930.
Coloured water paints on paper and cardboard, 40 x 57.4 cm. Paul Klee Foundation, Museum of Fine Arts, Bern.
© 1988 Cosmopress, Geneva.

Paul Klee (1879-1940)

Paul Klee focused on minute aspects of nature and from these developed the imaginary forms which were to inhabit his paintings. He created private symbols by fusing the real world with the world which existed in his mind.

In many of his paintings and drawings Klee has used lines to define shapes and lead our eye around the picture plane. The images of Klee's works exist in their own scale regardless of the real world. They are the result of his drawing explorations. Intimacy between the subject and the viewer is created on a minute scale. Klee used free associations to give life to his paintings, resulting in a virtually abstract style, which is often described as childlike.

The creative processes involved in making a work of art were of great importance to Klee, as he experimented freely in watercolour, pastel, ink, gouache and oil.

Throughout his career, Klee continued to search his imagination for inspiration, giving life to **imagistic** works of art.

In *Family Walk* by Paul Klee, for example, a few geometric shapes and edges are enough to represent the essential characteristics of human form in movement

Questions

1 Look closely at the drawing. How many human figures can you see in the drawing? How many animals?

2 In this work Klee has suggested movement with continuous lines. Follow the lines used with your eye or pencil. How many times do you have to lift your pencil off the page?

3 Experiment in representing images, for example, your classmates or animals using:
(a) continuous angular lines
(b) continuous curvilinear lines.

Line can be used to create the sensation of movement.

BRETT WHITELEY, *Divided Unity.*
Silkscreen print, two panels each 70 x 107 cm.
Bay Picture Library.

Brett Whiteley (born 1939)

Brett Whiteley is one of Australia's foremost contemporary artists and has also received international acclaim. Whiteley has expressed many themes in his work throughout his career. The themes and techniques vary depending on Whiteley's mood and intention. The sea allowed the emotional quality of Whiteley's style to dominate. The very personal quality of the brushwork in the series illustrates the influence of Eastern calligraphy. The forces of nature are overwhelming. The swirling lines suggest the shifting moods of the sea.

In this example, the continuous movement of turbulent air and water is emphasised by swirling brushwork. The variety of linework creates the effect of different types of movement – rough and choppy with short agitated brushstrokes and longer fluid brushstrokes to suggest the rising swell of a breaking wave.

Marcel Duchamp
(1887-1968)

Marcel Duchamp was a pioneer and experimenter during his artistic career. Throughout his career he became associated with different styles and movements of modern art due to his constant re-evaluation of his work. The movements ranged from Post-Impressionism, Cubism and Futurism to Dada. Cubism became a major influence during the period of 1911-1912.

Cubism analysed subjects and reinterpreted them from multiple shifting viewpoints. Colour was restricted to a limited range and there was a fine balance between recognisable images and abstract images. In this way, Cubism had a direct influence on Duchamp in *Nude Descending a Staircase No 2*. Duchamp, however, departed from the static quality of Cubism, transforming it into an entirely different style, which became known as Futurism. Movement was emphasised through graphic means.

Duchamp had a new approach to the subject. He has depicted a real person moving across a real environment. Dissecting planes move across the picture space representing the movement of the limbs of a body.

Nude Descending a Staircase caused great controversy and a new approach to art.

In this painting, the impression of a figure moving through space and time is created by the repetition of overlapping lines.

Jackson Pollock (1912-1956)

Jackson Pollock created his art work by splashing, dripping and throwing paint at the canvas. This is called **action painting.** The release of the artist's physical energy was more important than the end result. Action is more significant than representation.

MARCEL DUCHAMP, *Nude Descending a Staircase No. 2* 1912. Oil on canvas, 147.3 x 88.9 cm. Louise and Walter Arensberg Collection, Philadelphia Museum of Art.

Jackson Pollock was an American Abstract Expressionist artist who developed a painting style based on imagery from the unconscious.

The Abstract Expressionist movement emphasised the act of painting, the surface quality of the canvas, the importance of spontaneity and the creation of personal marks. The movement liberated the artist from traditional techniques of painting.

Pollock chose to create spontaneous paintings on unstretched canvas, usually tacked to the floor. In this way, Pollock felt directly involved with the work. Traditional tools such as brushes and easels were replaced by trowels, sand, fluid paint, sticks and knives.

The artist said: 'I have no fears about making changes, destroying the image because the painting has a life of its own'.

Action is needed to create line.

JACKSON POLLOCK, *Blue Poles* 1952.
Oil, synthetic polymer paint and aluminium paint, glass on canvas, 212 x 489 cm.
Collection: Australian National Gallery, Canberra.
© 1990 Pollock-Krasner Foundation. ARS N.Y.

In *Blue Poles* Jackson Pollock has created a large scale energetic painting which relies on line and movement for its effect. The painting demands a reaction from the spectator, provoking participation with the art work.

Never pre-planned, Pollock's work was influenced by Surrealism and Primitive art which depicted certain magical, natural and symbolic relationships. Navajo Indian sand painting was a particular influence on Pollock's work. These works were **ephemeral**. Their significance was in the creative processes involved in making them, rather than in representation.

Activity

1 Organise yourselves into small groups (outside if possible).
Each group will need a large piece of unstretched, unprimed canvas which should be laid on the ground.
Using your imagination, devise techniques of applying your paint to the canvas without traditional tools such as a brush and palette knife. Be as spontaneous as possible – don't plan the end result – just let it happen. Cover the entire canvas. Stretch the canvas when complete, if desired.

2 Compare and evaluate the results of your group with those of the other groups.

3 Now compare your end result to *Blue Poles*.

Chinese Landscape Painting

Chinese artists use a special type of brush called a brush pen to paint with – it has a bamboo handle, very soft hair and a very sharp point. It is also used for calligraphy – the art of writing in the Chinese language. How the brush is held, how much pressure is put on it and whether the brushstrokes are quick or slow determine the type of line created by the brush. Chinese paintings are usually painted on silk or rice paper, with black ink. The ink usually comes in the form of a dry block. The artist also has a block of slate, which is used like a palette, on which is placed an ink block and a little water. The ink block is ground with the water until the ink is dissolved and is dark enough. One other tool used by the Chinese artist is called a **chop** – it is a stamp made of marble in which the artist's name is carved. This is dipped into a pot of red wax and stamps the artist's name on the finished work. The Chinese chop indicates ownership. People who come into possession of an art work stamp it with their own chop to indicate their ownership of it.

In Chinese painting the special shadowing techniques used in landscapes to create details on mountains are called **wrinkles.** Chinese landscape painting developed and flourished considerably in the Five Dynasties period (907-960 AD) and the Northern Sung Dynasty (960-1127 AD) with three very influential schools of art headed by artists called Dong Yuan, Yi Chen, Fan Kuan and in the Southern Sung by Li Tang. Each artist developed a slightly different style influenced by the environment of his area of China.

Dong Yuan has smooth lines to represent low mountains, water and fields. He uses small dots to represent trees in a forest. The mountains have 'hemp' wrinkles.

Yi Chen is in northern China, which is a low dry landscape, occasionally washed by heavy rain or floods. His trees have drooping branches like crab claws. The clouds are curling and shadowy.

Fan Kuan in the northwest of China painted chains of big mountains with no trees. The mountains are detailed with 'dot' wrinkles.

Li Tang first lived in northern China, then moved to Hangzhou because the north was overrun by Mongols. His style is a combination of northern and southern styles with bold strokes and lots of ink. His shading technique has 'axe' wrinkles – it looks like they have been hacked out by an axe.

Throughout Chinese history, up until modern times, Chinese artists have been influenced by these styles of painting. Even today, many painters learn the traditional styles in art schools, while in some art schools it is the policy to combine the best characteristics from both Eastern and Western art. The latter is the case in the Zhejiang Fine Arts College in Hangzhou.

DONG YUAN STYLE

YI CHEN STYLE

FAN KUAN STYLE

LI TANG STYLE

Activity

One of the most important aims of the artist in a Chinese landscape painting is to create a pathway along which the viewer can travel through the painting. In this painting, the pathway the viewer can take is that of the water, as it moves from the top of the painting to the bottom. Find this pathway. Where does it start?

Now imagine you are in the painting, floating with the water and describe in detail your journey through the painting.

Your description should include: physical details, such as descriptions of rocks, trees, and the terrain over which you pass, as well as your feelings about what you encounter along the way.

雁蕩小龍湫乙丑夏耕雲畫於湘上

Professor Yao Gengyun, Contemporary Chinese Landscape Painting
Zhejiang Fine Arts College, Hangzhou.

Line may be used to describe states of feeling – emotional qualities.

EDVARD MUNCH, *The Scream* 1893.
Oil on cardboard, 91 x 73.5 cm.
Nasjonalgalleriet, Oslo.

Edvard Munch (1863-1944)

Munch wrote about *The Scream*: 'only someone insane could paint this!' At the time Munch was indeed in a severely psychologically disturbed state. He suffered from alcoholism which created dizziness and agoraphobia (fear of wide open spaces). Agoraphobics have a fear of being lost or swallowed up by the wide open spaces in the environment. The painting depicts the intensely distressing moment of anxiety when the figure hears a scream.

All the lines describing the fjord, plain, mountains and sky lead towards the focus, or point of interest in the artwork – the screaming head. The swirling lines, like sound waves, echo the anguish of the howling head.

Munch was fearful that he was going insane. He wrote in his diary about the experience that he depicts in the painting and lithograph:

'I was walking along the road with two friends. The sun set. I felt a tinge of melancholy. Suddenly the sky became a bloody red.

I stopped, leaned against the railing, dead tired, and looked at the flaming clouds that hung like blood and a sword over the blue-black fjord and the city.

My friends walked on. I stood there, trembling with fright. And I felt a great scream piercing nature.'

The artist can communicate feelings by using line **expressively**. Different types of lines encourage different emotional responses from the viewer.

'The things that fill my head and my heart must be expressed in my drawings and my paintings.'

Vincent Van Gogh

PABLO PICASSO, *Weeping Woman* 1937.
Oil on canvas, 59.7 x 48.9 cm. Tate Gallery, London.
© DACS 1988.

Questions

Look carefully at the painting.

1 Try to identify where both hands are in the picture.

2 What is she clutching in one hand?

3 Where are her tears? What do these shapes also represent?

Pablo Picasso (1881-1973)

Picasso was probably the most influential and formative artist of the 20th Century. His career lasted 75 years progressing through a wide range of styles, interests and themes, in a variety of media.

Picasso drew on events of his own life and his immediate surroundings for his subject matter. His work is mostly figurative – analysing, distorting and revealing the human form and condition, in its many-faceted aspects. His styles range from the **objective analysis** of his cubist works to the **subjective expressive distortions.**

The painting *Weeping Woman* depicts the suffering of a woman who has seen the horror of war. Picasso was extremely disturbed by the suffering and devastation caused by the indiscriminate bombing of a neutral Basque town called Guernica during the Spanish Civil War. He painted a monumental work called *Guernica* which portrays this event. He also developed a few smaller works on the same theme. *Weeping Woman* is one of them. The violent distortion created when Picasso combines two viewpoints of the face into one image as well as the dark, brutal, jagged lines communicate to us the intense distress of the woman.

PABLO PICASSO, *Sleeping Woman with Red Pillow* 1932.
Oil on canvas, 38 x 46 cm. Collection Marina Picasso.
Galerie Jan Krugier, Geneva.
© DACS 1988.

Using only a few fluid brushstrokes in *Sleeping Woman with Red Pillow,* Picasso depicted the firm, healthy figure of Marie-Thérèse, his mistress and model. His intention was to reveal simultaneously multiple viewpoints. In one image, he revealed her breasts and buttocks. The areas of colour surrounding the figure don't reveal any particular viewpoint or form. The flowing curvilinear lines create a form which suggests peacefulness.

Questions

1 Picasso loved his model Marie-Thérèse. What aspects of her physical being and personality did Picasso try to depict?

2 Choose an object (or person) in the art room and draw it in such a way that you can see more than one view of it in your drawing.

PABLO PICASSO, *Nude in a Rocking Chair* 1956.
Oil on canvas, 195 x 130 cm.
Purchased 1981.
Collection: Art Gallery of New South Wales
© DACS 1988.

In his later work, such as *Nude in a Rocking Chair*, Picasso treated his forms with an abandoned fierceness and grotesqueness. His brushwork is painterly, calligraphic and brutal.

Picasso's representations of the female form reveal, in their various styles, the influence of the artist's life on his paintings. In the *Nude in a Rocking Chair*, the figure is disintegrated, shattered and aggressive.

Questions

1 Why does Picasso use a black outline around the figure?

2 What sort of lines has he used to describe the figure?

3 What mood does this create?

14

Aboriginal Art

Aboriginal artists approach their work with a different philosophy to Western artists. Western artists usually depict their own personal experiences and ideas. In Aboriginal art, however, design and motifs are culturally standardised, representing the collective experience and traditions of the whole race.

Aboriginal art usually has religious significance and is used for ceremonial purposes. It is a means of communicating information about religious beliefs. Their art frequently relates to Dreamtime beliefs. In the Dreamtime, the shape of the world as we know it and all the living things that inhabit it were created. They believe the force of Dreamtime beings are still hidden within the land.

In their rituals and ceremonies, Aboriginals re-enact the events of the Dreamtime. The making of art objects is part of the ritual calling on the spiritual powers of the Dreamtime beings. Most designs and images on art objects, stories, songs, and dances belong to different Aboriginal groups. Each group owns the stories, or images, and no other group is allowed to use them without permission.

Aboriginal paintings can be found in many places on different types of surfaces. Two of the main types are **rock paintings** and **bark paintings.** Much of the bark painting is found in an area of northern Australia called Arnhem Land and there seems to be two main styles. One style we call **figurative** because it represents the figures of animals, birds, reptiles and humans. It usually has a plain ochre background on which is painted the X-ray images of the figures so that internal as well as external details are visible. Sometimes the images are covered with a pattern of straight lines. The second style is **geometric** and **abstract** because the whole surface of the bark is broken up into sections in a geometric pattern using dividing lines. Figurative images, geometric shapes, dots and lines fill each section of the paintings. The figurative style is usually found in western Arnhem Land and the geometric style in north-eastern Arnhem Land.

Hand stencil.
Murawijinnie Caves, Nullarbor Plains.
Courtesy Aboriginal Heritage Branch, South Australia.

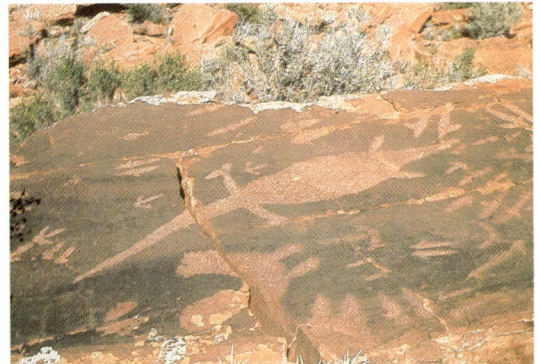

Rock engraving.
Eucolo Creek, near Woomera.
Courtesy Aboriginal Heritage Branch, South Australia.

Questions

In Aboriginal art, images are represented by symbols and signs. They are personal, can tell a story and can be used to create pattern.

1 What symbols do **we** use in our lives to represent objects or events?
Write down some well-known ones.
You may have personal symbols that have meaning only to yourself, that are secret, just as they are in Aboriginal art. Write these down too.

2 In three panels on a piece of art paper, tell a story using symbols and signs of your own choosing, about your home, your journey to school, and your time at school.

15

Line can be used to create **pattern**.

GEORGE GARRAWUN, Djinang born 1944, *Freshwater fish* 1979.
Ochres on eucalyptus bark, 158.5 x 74.0 cm
Collection: Australian National Gallery, Canberra.
Licence granted by Aboriginal Artists Agency, North Sydney.

Line used in Sculpture

A sculptor can 'draw' with line through real space using materials such as wire.

ALEXANDER CALDER, *Romulus and Remus* 1928.
Wire sculpture. Photograph: David Heald.
Collection: The Solomon R Guggenheim Museum, New York.

Alexander Calder (1898-1976)

The development of Calder's sculpture was greatly influenced by his early technological studies in mathematics, technical drafting, mechanics and engineering.

Early in his career, Calder progressed into wire sculpture. *Romulus and Remus* (1928) is an example from this period. Calder's interest in the Surrealist art of Miro, Klee and Picasso was evident in this first stage of his career.

From 1930 to 1933 Calder developed an entirely new form of abstract sculpture based on motion – mobiles. He has used many materials. His mobiles can be divided into three categories: standing, wall and hanging. Some of his earlier mobiles incorporated found objects, such as bits of coloured glass and pottery; and free-form pieces of carved wood. Later, they were made of metal and were in primary colours – red, yellow and blue; plus black and white. His later works were made of steel. The mobiles move in particularly complex ways, having parts that move up and down, as well as rotating, to form infinitely varied patterns in space.

ALEXANDER CALDER, *Antennae with Red and Blue Dots* 1960.
Kinetic metal sculpture. Tate Gallery, London.

Calder plans his mobiles using scale models, cutting the shapes from light aluminium and rearranging the shapes until they create an interesting pattern that is balanced. Calder's mobiles are free to move with the slightest hint of breeze or moving air. They have a bright, playful mood about them that reminds us of the paintings of Miro and Klee.

The third stage of Calder's work saw the introduction of **stabiles.** Monumental organic forms were devised using mathematical and scientific knowledge. Calder combined organic forms with technological knowledge to create a new outlook in 20th Century sculpture.

Robert Klippel (born 1920)

Klippel, from the beginning of his career as an artist, was interested in both figurative and non-figurative sculpture. He was interested in natural forms and machinery – he explored both the mechanical workings of machines and the organic growth patterns in nature. An early example, *Entities Suspended from a Detector* (1948) is an example of his interest in the relationship between mechanised and organic forms.

Later Klippel became more involved with **open sculpture** in which **space** was an important element. He began to use metal after he had learnt how to weld. He created delicate works with rods and thin metal sheets. Gradually his work became extremely complex and mechanistic and he began to incorporate junk metal, discarded machine pieces, into his works.

Metal Sculpture Opus No 250 (1970) can be described as **linear** because the sculpture emphasises lines which draw a pattern in space. In this work the emphasis is on space (void) as a major visual element rather than mass (solid). The mechanical shapes penetrate an area of space which is enclosed within a frame of metal.

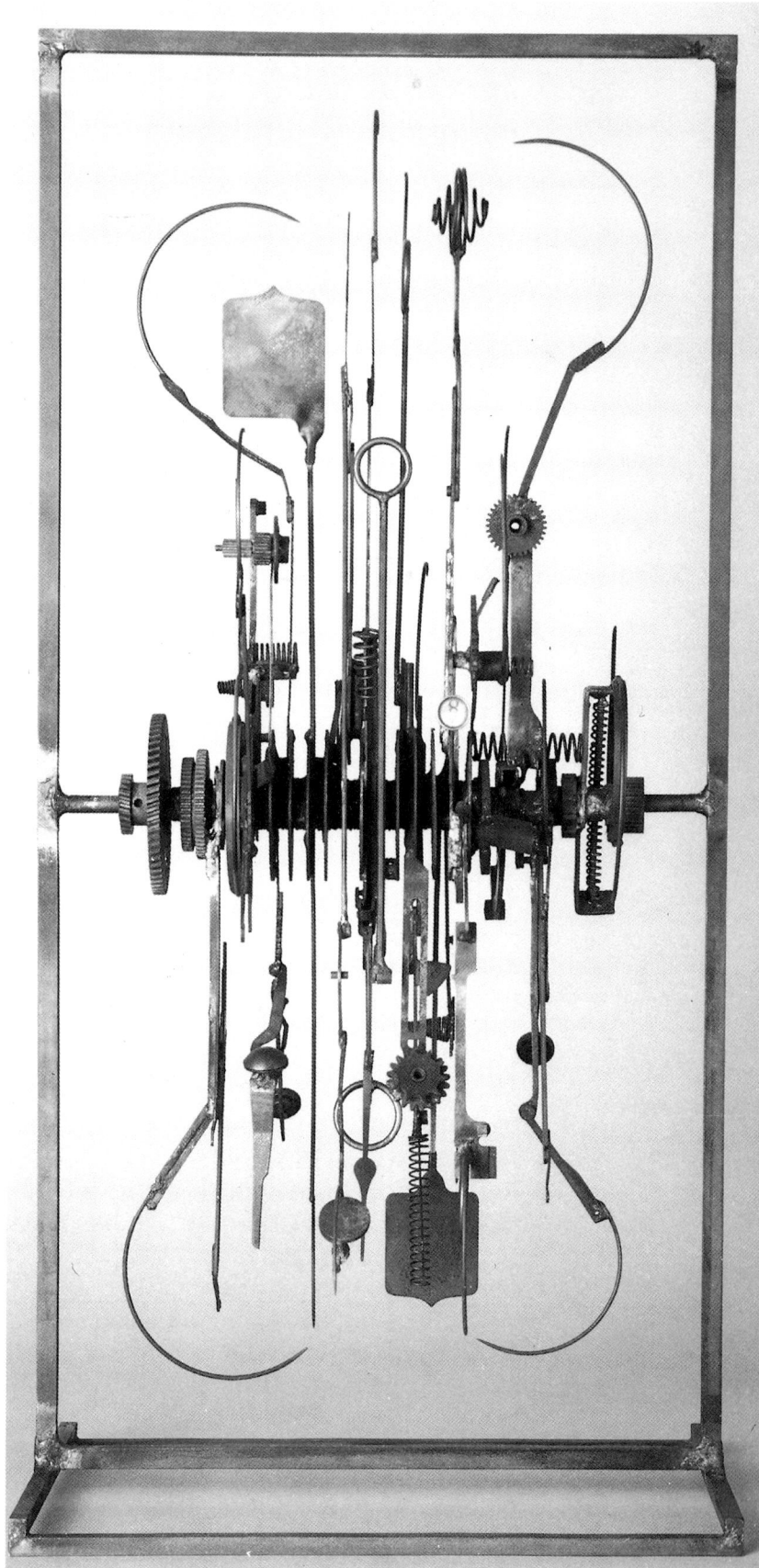

ROBERT KLIPPEL, *Metal Sculpture opus No. 250* 1970.
Brazed and welded metal, 64.7 x 31.2 x 26 cm.
Collection: Australian National Gallery, Canberra.

There are many different **types** of lines – curved, straight, thick, thin, wiggly, jagged, wavy, curly, broken, etc. Lines can be created with many different materials:

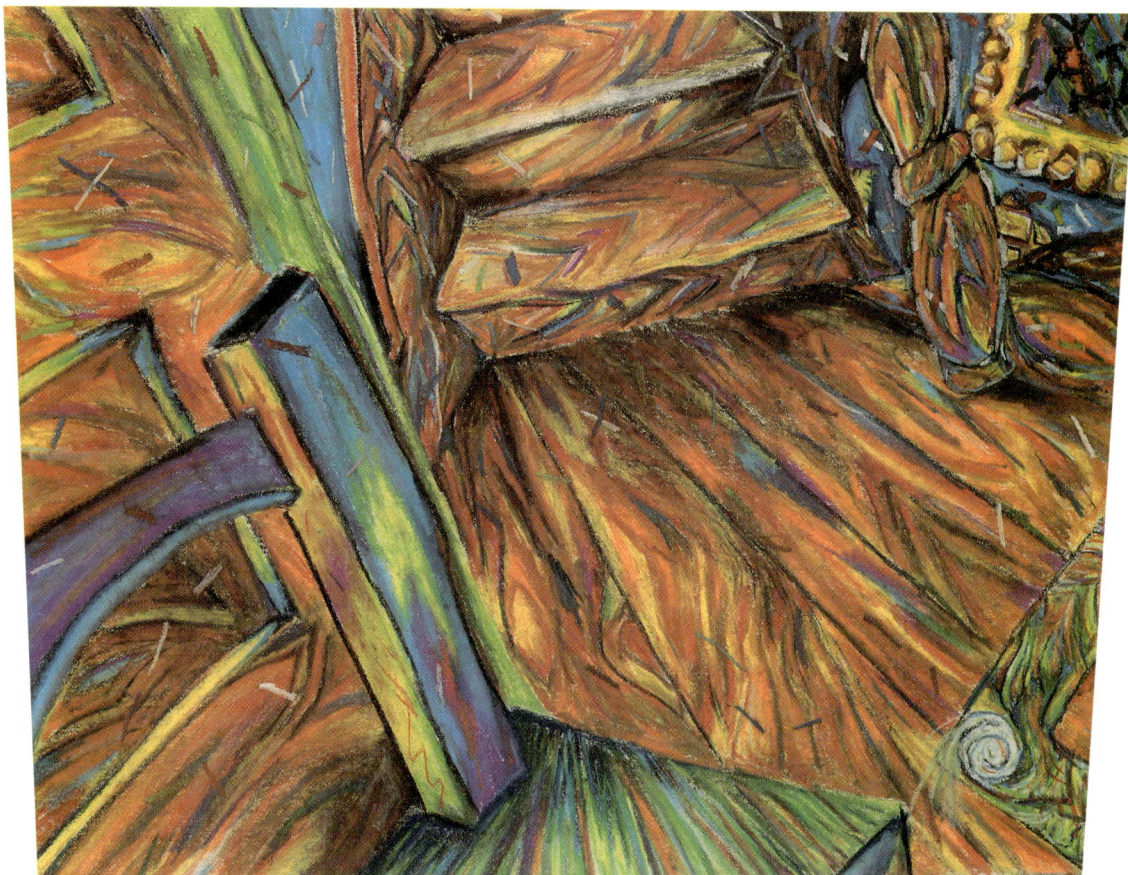

STEVEN SCOTT, student.

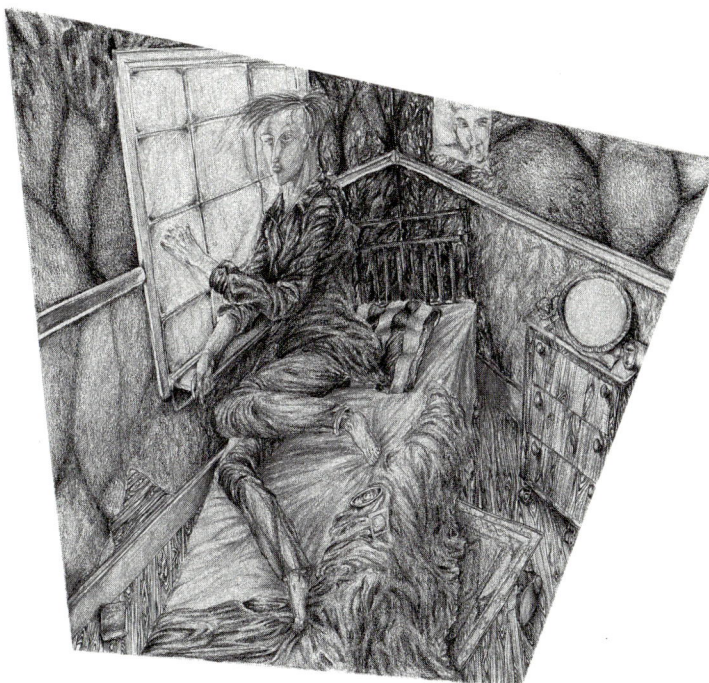

STEVEN SCOTT, student.

19

Experimenting with Line

Activity

1 Draw up a grid in your sketchbook or on a sheet of art paper, with at least eight spaces or boxes. Using as many **different drawing materials** as you can find, experiment with various types of line and see how the effect changes when using different drawing materials. Write underneath each box the **descriptive** words you would use to explain the types of lines you have created and the materials you have used.

2 **Blind contour drawing:** Using a fine black felt pen and a sheet of paper, draw your own hand or a classmate's hand from direct observation. Students should look at the subject intently, but **not** look at the paper while the pen is moving. Imagine that the point of your pen is actually touching the inner and outer edges, or **contour,** of the form and that your eyes and the point of the pen are moving together to show every subtle change of direction.

3 **Contour drawing:** Use the same method as in exercise 2, but this time you can look at the page as you draw and relate each form to the next.

4 **Observation drawing:** Using black felt tip pens again draw a full figure of one of your classmates; this time try to draw all the details. Think carefully about body shapes and directions. Where can you bend your body, arms and legs? Have you indicated that in your drawings? Using this method with other objects and forms in the classroom, learn to look carefully at the objects you draw. Compare the development of your drawings. Discuss results with other class members and your teacher. Have your drawings improved? Why/why not?

5 Using only a pen or fine-point texta, draw an object from somewhere in the art room, such as a pencil sharpener, tap, bench vice; or a small section of your clothing, for example, creases and cuff of shirt.

Draw this object (or a part of it) larger than life so that it fills the whole page of a sketchbook or a small sheet of art paper. Use line to emphasise the details and to create the effect of shadows falling on the object.

6 Using wax crayon, cover an entire sheet of art paper with a variety of colours. Paint over the crayon with black paint. When the paper is dry, etch through the surface using a pointed tool, such as the end of a compass, to create different types of lines to represent images. Experiment with the size and direction of lines to create areas of light and pattern.

Focus areas could include views of the art room or the playground.

Shape

Shapes can be enclosed by a line but shapes can be created *without* lines. Shapes can be **geometric** or **organic**.

JOHN COBURN, *Primordial Garden* 1965-1966.
Liquitex on hardboard, 157.6 x 122.3 cm. Felton Bequest 1968.
National Gallery of Victoria.

Organic shapes remind us of the natural world in which objects are usually irregular, uneven and constantly changing. They are usually curvilinear or curve-edged.

John Coburn (born 1925)

Coburn's work is characterised by organic shapes that appear to be simplifications of plant forms. They are flat and exist in a very shallow spatial plane on the surface of the canvas. The shapes have razor-sharp edges possibly stimulated by American art which was given labels such as **hard-edge, flat-area abstraction, minimal art** and **colour field painting.** The range of colours chosen by Coburn is usually minimal – broad areas of flat colour. Coburn's later work became even more abstract and simplified – the flat shapes existing in only one plane – not overlapping.

Coburn's *Curtain of the Sun* decorates the southern end of the Opera Theatre in the Sydney Opera House. He chose warm yellows, reds, pinks and browns for this woven tapestry curtain. His *Curtain of the Moon* in the Drama Theatre has deep blues, greens and browns.

Shape is a two-dimensional **area** surrounded by **space.** A three-dimensional shape is called a **form** – it can be a solid **mass** or an enclosed **volume** of space (like a glass box). A form can be penetrated by space or voids.

Geometric shapes remind us of the precision of man-made or mechanical objects. They are usually rectilinear or straight-edged.

Kasimir Malevich
(1878-1935)

A Russian artist, who like the Italian Futurists, became involved in praising the machine-age and rejecting the past. Malevich's art was a kind of pure, geometrical abstraction – a total break from reality. He gave his style of art the name Suprematism. He first experimented with some elements of the styles of Cubism and Futurism, but finally settled on a form of art that was totally free from subject matter (that is his art does not represent any object or figure) it is purely abstract.

In his later works, even the squares and rectangles almost disappeared, as he simplified and abstracted his works to a simple square on a square – sometimes a black square on white and later a white tilted square on a square white canvas.

KASIMIR MALEVICH, *House Under Construction* 1915-1916. Oil on canvas, 96.6 x 44 cm. Collection: Australian National Gallery, Canberra.

Two-dimensional shapes can be recreated in the three-dimensional form of sculpture. The areas of space enclosed by the arrangement of shapes are an equally important part of the organisation of the sculpture.

David Smith (1906-1965)

The sculptural works by David Smith are in some ways like the paintings by Kasimir Malevich. They are mostly geometric and abstract. This work called *25 Planes* is assembled or constructed from flat metal pieces. Smith learned to weld metal in an automobile factory in 1925. He worked on sculptures made from a variety of metals.

Smith's early works were very linear – they were like drawings in space. For a while his work was figurative in derivation. Later they became more abstract. His latest work was constructed of stainless steel which was polished then abraded.

25 Planes is presented basically as a two-dimensional piece to be viewed from the front, however the viewer can walk around the art work. Smith invites the viewer's eye to move through space following the diagonally placed **planes.** The rectangular and square forms of this sculpture are arranged in space. The surface of the planes are also 'alive' with the movement of light where it hits the scratchings that are carved into the polished surface of each plane. The line or path created by the planes is full of energy – the different lengths of the planes, the intervals and the pauses in the movement along the path are something like a piece of music.

DAVID SMITH, *25 Planes* 1958.
Stainless steel, 350.5 x 169.5 x 40 cm.
Collection: Australian National Gallery.

Henry Moore (1898-1986)

Henry Moore created organic forms in his sculptures. Most sculptures are abstracted to various extents and are often based on figures. The sculptures reflect the great interest Moore had in the quality of the material being used,

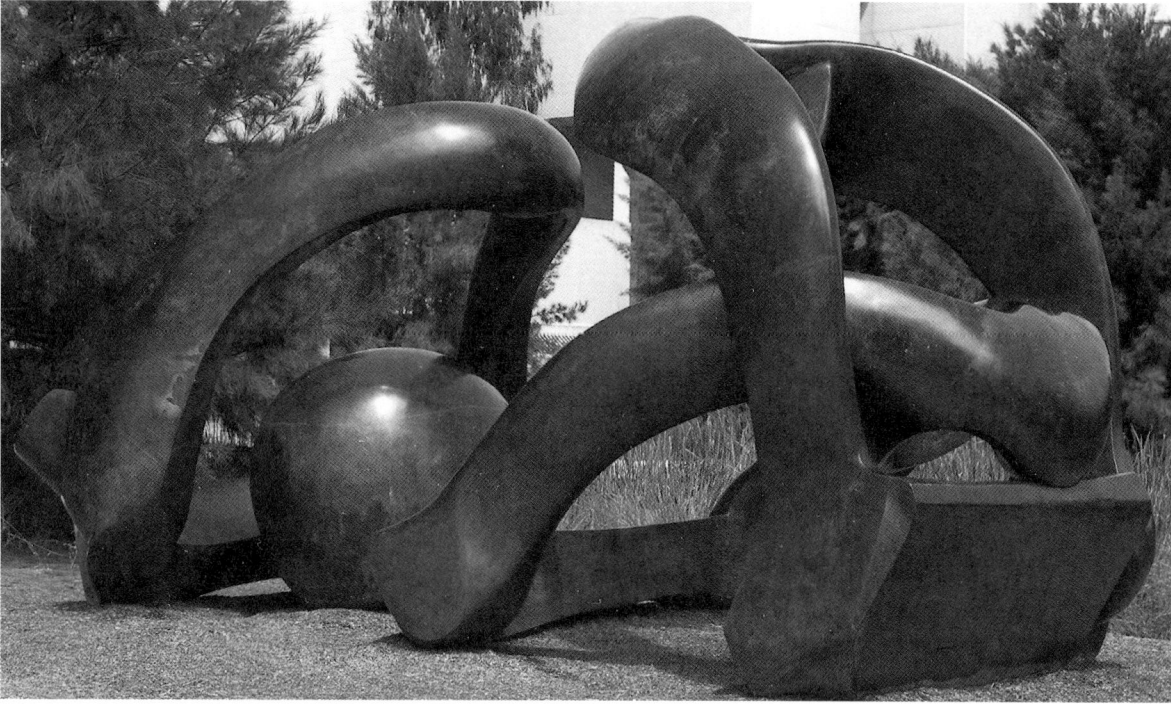

HENRY MOORE, *Hill Arches* 1973.
Bronze, 247 x 548 x 247 cm, cast 1973 by Noack Foundry, Berlin. No. 4 of an edition of four.
Collection: Australian National Gallery, Canberra.

whether it was bronze, stone, wood or plaster.

Moore had a preference for **direct carving,** however some works are **cast** and others are **constructed.**

Many of Moore's sculptures are of a large scale adding weight and intensity to their effect on the viewer. They were often designed to be viewed in direct relationship to the outdoor environment, giving the impression they have been weathered by the elements. Henry Moore greatly influenced sculpture through his use of pierced forms, interest in surface texture and use of organic forms.

HENRY MOORE, *Reclining Nude* 1937.
Bronze, 10.48 x 21.6 cm. Gift of Mr and Mrs Albert Lion.
Baltimore Museum of Art, BMA 1955.62.

The geometry and precision of our man-made landscape is often the subject of contemporary painters. This work emphasises the sharp regularity of man-made forms. Horizontal and vertical lines dominate this landscape.

JEFFREY SMART, *Corrugated Giaconda* c 1976.
Oil on canvas, 81 x 116 cm. Collection: Australian National Gallery, Canberra.

Jeffrey Smart (born 1921)

Jeffrey Smart is a painter of the urban landscape – highrise buildings, corrugated fences, motor-cars, trucks, street signs – usually including an isolated figure frozen in the midst of his man-made environment. The paintings are sharp, clear and photographically realistic. Yet his works have an air of mystery, perhaps because the landscapes and figures seem to exist in a world totally without atmosphere or movement. In Smart's paintings the elements are always carefully and painstakingly composed in the classical sense. Regardless of Smart's modernistic approach he believes totally in the importance of composition in designing a painting. Smart places the shapes and colours in his paintings in a balanced and geometrically organised way on the canvas. It is also important to note the presence in all Smart's work either of figures or of evidence of man in the form of man-made objects.

Ken Done

Ken Done expresses the vibrance, colour, and mood of the Australian environment in his paintings and drawings. Shapes are often extremely simplified to create a direct and almost childlike suggestion of the scenery. The works possess a spontaneous quality with bold sweeping brush and pencil work. Bright areas of flat colour, bold outlines and thickly applied areas of paint create a decorative approach intended to delight the senses.

KEN DONE, *November Lilies* 1986.
Ink on paper, 55 x 74 cm. Art Directors Gallery, Sydney.

KEN DONE, *Frangipani* 1984.
Silkscreen, 51 x 65 cm. Art Directors Gallery, Sydney.

Shape in Architecture

Some architectural designers envisage their buildings as sculptural forms – an arrangement of shapes that enclose space. The buildings embody the ideas and feelings of the designer or symbolise its function.

Gerrit Rietveld (1888-1964)

Schroeder House in Utrecht is the physical translation into architecture of the theoretical ideas of a movement of artists in Holland called De Stijl. This group of artists aimed for the collaboration of artists in developing a philosophy that was common to painters, sculptors, architects, and graphic and industrial designers. Their work emphasised simplicity, clarity, mathematical order and structure, principally all through the use of the straight line.

Schroeder House uses rectilinear forms that are a translation of the paintings of Piet Mondrian. In architecture as in painting, colours were simplified to simple primaries (red, yellow, blue) and neutrals (black, white, grey).

Fritz Wotruba (1907-1975)

This church, built from reinforced concrete, could be described almost as a monumental piece of sculpture more than a building. It is an arrangement of massive cubic forms which suggests more of a chance arrangement of children's building blocks than a functional organisation of building materials. Here we see the architect more as a sculptor than as engineer. The structure and materials of this building may be seen as embodying the solidity and stability of the Christian religion. The church is a monument suggesting the enduring spirit of Christianity.

GERRIT RIETVELD, Schroeder House 1923-1924, Utrecht, The Netherlands

FRITZ WOTRUBA, Church of the Holy Trinity 1965-1976, Vienna, Austria.

FRANK LLOYD WRIGHT, Solomon R Guggenheim Museum 1943-1946, 1956-1959.
Photograph: David Heald. Collection: Solomon R Guggenheim Museum, New York.

Frank Lloyd Wright
(1869-1959)

Frank Lloyd Wright conceived the Guggenheim Museum as a continuous flowing form. To achieve this he created a spiral ramp which is part of the main structure of the building. This spiral ramp encircles a huge central space five times between the top of the building and the ground. As the ramp winds its way down the radius of the circle decreases.

Paintings displayed within the museum are illuminated by light which enters through glazed spaces between the levels of the ramp and from a large transparent dome spanning the centre of the building.

Due to the unusual inclination of the ramp, the inner walls of the building allow paintings to be exhibited as though viewed on an easel. Whilst viewing the works, the spectator slowly descends the building.

This huge spiral construction resembles an organic form contrasting starkly with the angular nature of the surrounding buildings in its city environment.

Experiments with Shape

Print design using three stencils

1 Using geometric rectilinear shapes or curvilinear organic shapes or a combination of both, cut three separate stencils with shapes organised in different ways on each sheet of art paper. Keep the pieces you have cut out for the following exercise.

You can print this design on a white or coloured surface. To print your shapes, simply sponge or roll paint over the surface of the paper stencil so that the paint goes through the cut-out areas. When the first print is dry, print the following two stencils. Try to experiment with a variety of colours and tones.

2 Using the pieces you cut from the three paper stencils, arrange the shapes on a white or coloured surface. Print a negative print pattern by sponging or rolling paint onto the surface around the shapes. Remove the shapes and rearrange them to overlap some of the original areas and print with a different colour.

Abstract design using the alphabet

1 Using a ruler draw up a rectangular frame. Divide this area into at least five bands of equal or unequal spacing.

2 Carefully draw up the letters of the alphabet along these lines. Use all the space available. Allow the letters to touch. Remember you are not writing a message but are creating new shapes.

3 Paint each new shape. Select colours carefully. Avoid outlining the letters.

Relief-print using imaginative shapes

1 Using a sheet of manila cardboard draw a variety of different sized shapes. Experiment with combinations of straight and curved edged shapes. The limit is your imagination. The shapes may be loosely related to living creatures, plant forms, moon shapes etc, or the shapes may be inspired by man-made images such as signs or letters.

2 Cut these shapes out carefully with a stencil knife or scissors and glue them securely to another piece of thicker cardboard. Try different arrangements by overlapping shapes

and organising each shape onto different levels.

3 Paint evenly with a layer of shellac on both sides and allow to dry (this step is necessary only when more than one or two prints are desired). When dry cover the surface of the cardboard relief evenly with lino printing ink and roller. Print the design onto paper using a press or by applying equal pressure from the back by hand.

Cut Paper Design

Draw up a large rectangular frame. Cut out three large irregular shapes (they may be curved or straight edged) and arrange in their own space within the frame. Paint the background space formed. Using additional coloured paper cut out different types of imaginary shapes of varying sizes and organise on top of the existing design. Try to overlap the shapes and interconnect the shapes, leading the viewers eye in different directions. The shapes may appear to be floating. Decide carefully where you place each colour.

You may look at the paper designs of Henri Matisse for inspiration or the floating shapes which exist in the paintings of Paul Klee.

Remember that a successful design should look balanced from any angle.

Organic/Geometric Design

1 Using coloured cardboard, paper or printed paper from magazines cut out a number of curvilinear organic shapes or rectilinear geometric shapes and arrange in an interesting combination on a large sheet of art paper.

2 With a pencil extend the outlines of these shapes to the edges of the paper creating a network of lines on the paper.

3 Paint the spaces that are created with lighter or darker shades of warm or cool colours.

Design based on found object

1 Select an object from your immediate environment either at home or at school. The object may be a kitchen utensil, a piece of art equipment, a piece of machinery, furniture or an electrical appliance.

2 Draw the different parts of this object and reconstruct to create an interesting combination of shapes.

3 Extend the visual information by experimenting with linework to create interesting patterns. Try repeating lines to build up a feeling of movement or rhythm. Break up larger shapes with smaller shapes. Allow the design to grow or evolve gradually. Try to combine the skills learnt in the line and shape units

KATE MARTIN, student.

Tone

Tone is the degree of **lightness** or **darkness** of a colour. A **tint** is produced when white is added to a colour to make it **lighter**. A **shade** is produced when black is added to a colour to make it **darker**.

JOHN BRACK, *The Car* 1955.
Oil on canvas, 41 x 101.8 cm. Purchased 1956.
National Gallery of Victoria.

The use of light tone with a dark tone creates a **contrast** which serves the purpose of emphasising the shapes or forms.

John Brack (born 1920)

During the 1950s and 1960s John Brack presented a close look at institutions of Australian life – the family, the city and suburban dreariness. He depicted the common experience of life in the cities and suburbs. Prosperity was growing and with it grew a new breed of consumers.

In *The Car* an uneasy mood is created by the limited range of colours, the static quality of the human images and the **strong tonal contrast.** The family inside the car are presented as stark contrasts to the exterior world. They exist as a silhouette protected inside the car from a harsh Australian environment. However, the faces of the family possess the same harsh quality staring out at the viewer with rigid features.

The paintings from this period of John Brack's career are clearly-organised, figurative works. Many of his works make a pessimistic comment about society.

The gradation of tonal values from light to dark can be used to create the illusion of volume (three-dimensional forms) on a two-dimensional surface such as paper or canvas. This effect was called **chiaroscuro** by the Italians – literally 'chiaro' light and 'scuro' dark.

WILLIAM DOBELL, *Margaret Olley* 1948.
Oil on hardboard, 114.3 x 85.7 cm. Purchased 1949.
Collection: Art Gallery of New South Wales.
Reproduced by permission of the William Dobell Foundation.

William Dobell (1899-1970)

Dobell's portrait of *Margaret Olley* won the 1948 Archibald Prize for portraiture. The Archibald Prize was set up by a bequest in the will of Jules Francois Archibald who died in 1919. The prize is judged every year by the trustees of the Art Gallery of New South Wales for the best portrait '. . . of some man or woman distinguished in art, letters, science or politics'.

Dobell's earlier winning portrait of *Joshua Smith* in 1943 created a stir amongst some disgruntled entrants in the competition, who took Dobell and the trustees to court. They claimed that

Dobell's representation of Joshua Smith was not a 'portrait', but rather a caricature due to its exaggeration and elongation of the figure.

The portrait of *Margaret Olley* also exaggerated certain features of her figure, in particular her voluptuous roundness. One of Dobell's aims was to represent not only the physical characteristics of the person but also the essential characteristics of their personality. The portrait creates an impression of Margaret Olley as a pleasant and happy soul.

GEORGES BRAQUE, *Houses and Trees* 1909.
Oil on canvas, 65.5 x 54 cm. Purchased 1980.
Collection: Art Gallery of New South Wales.
©ADAGP, Paris/DACS, London 1988.

Georges Braque (1882-1963)

Picasso and Braque were cofounders of the Cubist movement which began during 1907. The main aim of Picasso and Braque was the **analysis of form.** They had been influenced by primitive African art, archaic sculpture and the theories of the post Impressionist artist Cezanne.

In *Houses and Trees,* colour has been reduced to tones of earthy greens, ochres and browns to emphasise the formal structure of the subject. The houses and trees have been reduced to their basic three dimensional forms. Using block-like forms the artist represents the trees and houses in terms of volumes. They possess a crystalline quality.

The atmosphere and perspective of a realistic landscape view has been replaced with an imaginative scene. Objects are analysed from different viewpoints and are manipulated or restructured to create geometric structures. The viewer is able to piece together essential forms as they are organised in the confined space of the picture surface. The carefully ordered surface of the painting is textured with obvious brushstrokes.

This style of painting is called Analytical Cubism. The Cubist movement freed artists from merely reproducing naturalistic representations of nature.

Chuck Close (born 1940)

During the late 1960s and early 1970s the art world saw a return to precise observation in art or Realism. These artists became known as the Photo Realists because they used the photograph as a reference point. They painstakingly recorded illusions of photographs of commonplace subjects taken from their own environment.

In the late 1960s Chuck Close began placing certain restrictions on his painting. He chose familiar images such as close friends and began painting a series of large scale portraits starting with a self-portrait. These paintings are simply known by the person's first name, for example *Phil 1969* and *Portrait of Bob.*

Chuck Close enjoyed the limitations of photographs of people's heads. These permit him to zoom in and study detail and experiment with surface textures, focus and distance.

Initially Close painted only in black and white, however he later developed his own colour schemes limited to about three colours. A grid technique was used by Close to transfer information from the photograph to the canvas applying the paint with an airbrush. Works on paper are painted with ink or water colour, for example *Leslie 1973.*

The Photo Realist artists placed little importance on the actual subject with greater concern placed on the painting technique.

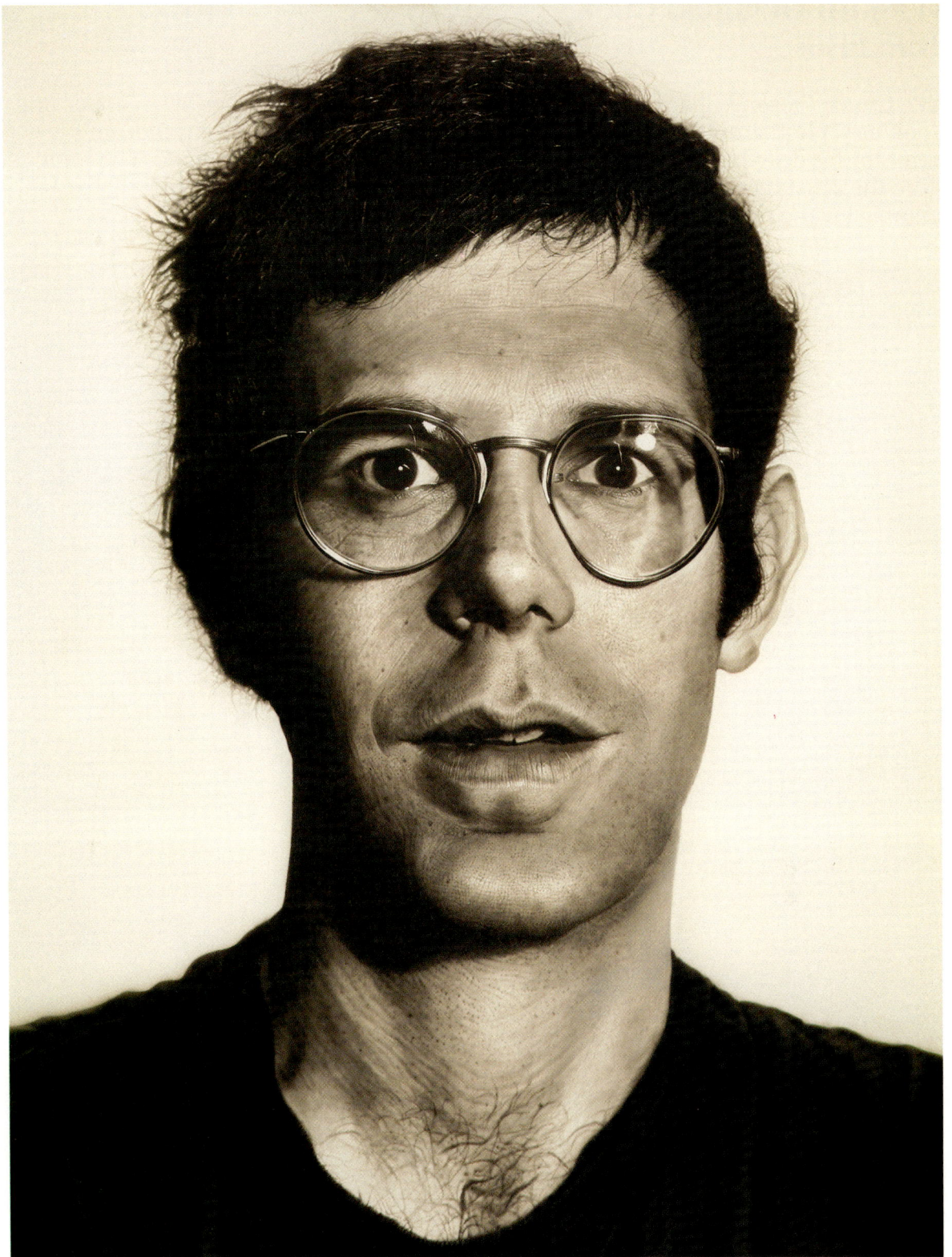

CHUCK CLOSE, *Bob* 1970.
Synthetic polymer paint on canvas, 274.5 x 213.5 cm.
Collection: Australian National Gallery, Canberra.

William Delafield Cook
(born 1936)

Like Chuck Close, William Delafield Cook uses photographs as a starting point for his drawings and paintings. Here the artist has selected a subject suitable for the medium of charcoal and conte crayon on paper over canvas and transferred the information from his photograph to the drawing. The tonal accuracy is reflected in this still life drawing.

WILLIAM DELAFIELD COOK, *Pumpkin* 1977.
Charcoal and black conte, 60.8 x 71 cm. Purchased 1977.
National Gallery of Victoria.

Experiments with Tone

The impression of light and shade can be created in a variety of drawing and painting materials. For example: A soft 2B pencil can create the effect of a gradual tonal change from light to dark. Other techniques can also be used with drawing implements such as pen or texta.

Exercises

1 Using a grid try to create the effect of a light to dark gradation using a drawing material of your choice.

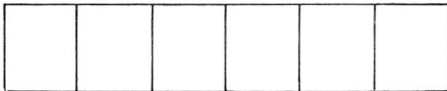

light   dark

2 Look through newspapers and magazines to find and collect examples of different techniques used by artists to create the effect of tone. Stick these in your sketchbook.

3 Using a pen or finepoint texta draw an object from somewhere in the art room, such as a pencil sharpener, tap or bench vice. Draw it larger than life if it is very small and use the cross-hatching method to create tonal values.

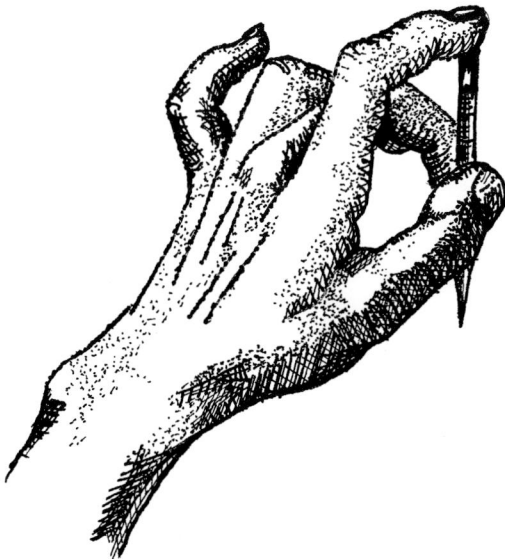

4 Find another interesting object or an area of the art room. You are going to 'draw' this using a brush and wash in only one colour (monochrome). Use only water to lighten your colour. Look for dark, mid and light tones. When your painting is dry, use a fine point texta to emphasise certain dominant lines and darker tonal areas.

5 Select a range of commercial packages such as junk food containers and packets, aluminium drink cans, chocolate bar wrappers or lollies. Look closely at their design. Look at areas of light and shadow. The edges closest to us reflect light. These will be depicted lightest. Experiment with reproducing the surface in light and dark shading to create different areas of tone. Use a variety of drawing materials, for example charcoal, conte crayon or fine point texta.

6 Sketch a figure study of a member of your class or family. Choose a relaxed position for the sitter. Look at areas of the body and clothing which reflect the light. These will be the lightest areas of your drawing. Next, experiment with layers of soft ink wash to build up the sections of shadow. To create the darkest shadows use several overlapping washes. Look closely at the qualities of the clothing which can be represented by details of light and shadow, such as folds, stitching, patterns or buttons.

7 Select a photograph of yourself, a relative or friend, preferably in black and white. Rule up a pencil grid on the photograph dividing it into equal squares. On a separate sheet of drawing paper draw a second grid with the same number of squares (these could be slightly larger). Look closely at the areas of light and dark in each square on the photograph. Reproduce these light and dark sections using soft pencil shading in the corresponding squares on your grid.

Gradually add the information into each square, making sure your shading always corresponds to the shading on the photograph.

Avoid using outlines. You are drawing with tones. Watch the face appear in light and shadow.

8 Look for areas in your home or school environment which represent opportunities to extend into drawings which describe different qualities of light and dark on different surfaces.

(a) At home — in the kitchen, in your wardrobe, in your bedroom.

(b) At school — any viewpoint of the classroom — the art room sink and window sill.

Experiment with different drawing materials and techniques to build up darker areas and lighter areas. Reproduce light and dark areas by mixing light and dark tones with paint.

Homework Assignment

Create a series of drawings based on man-made and natural objects. Emphasise the different areas of light and shadow on the surface of the objects. Which direction is the light coming from as it strikes the surface of the object?

Man-made subjects could include household appliances such as irons, saucepans, the kitchen sink, garden hose and tap.

Natural subjects could include fruit, vegetables, plants, shells or seedpods.

Texture

Texture is how the surface of an object feels to touch – rough, lumpy, prickly, scaly, hairy, slippery and so on. This is **real texture** and is an important element in sculpture. In painting the surface of the canvas could actually be textured due to thick application of paint or perhaps addition of other materials to the surface such as sand, hessian, newsprint and so on. The illusion of texture can also be created in painting by imitating the texture pattern using dots, lines and scratches. This is called **simulated texture.**

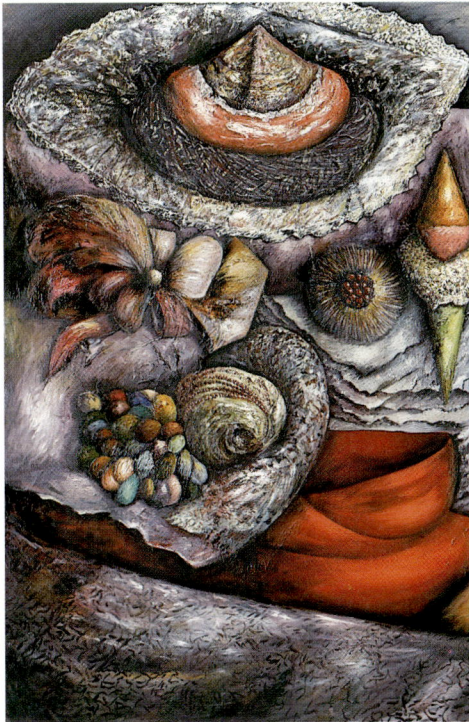

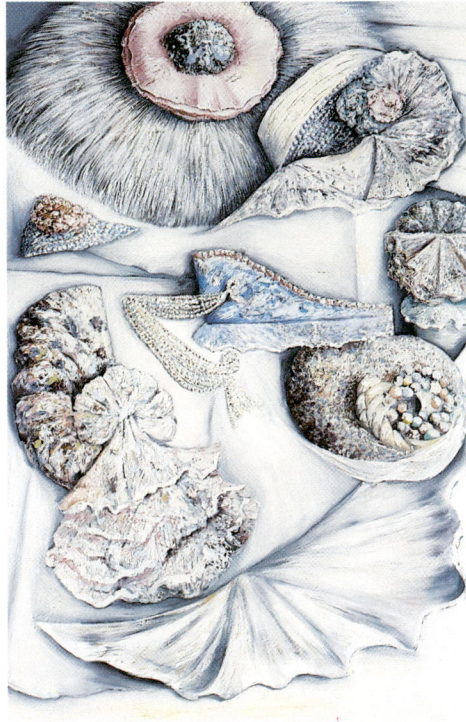

SUSAN NORRIE, *Fruitful Corsage; Bridal Bouquet; Lingering Veils* 1983.
Oil on canvas, 182 x 121 cm (each panel).
Purchased with Henry Salkauskas Contemporary Art Purchase Fund 1983.
Collection: Art Gallery of New South Wales.

Susan Norrie (born 1953)

Susan Norrie has made a significant impact on Australian art of the 1980s. Her paintings introduce powerful imagery and the values of a female artist. The images selected focus on feminine lifestyle, a previously unexplored subject in Australian Art.

The triptych *Fruitful Corsage; Bridal Bouquet; Lingering Veils* is Susan Norrie's first large scale major painting to be selected by the New South Wales Art Gallery. In depicting personal still life imagery, Norrie experiments with the surface quality of the painting. A very detailed observation of each personal object is evident as well as a sensitivity to its uniqueness. Flowers, jewellery, materials and ornaments become preciously encrusted with thickly textured paint. Each object is infused with a life of its own built up by richly coloured paint and a wide range of textural effects.

COLIN LANCELEY, *Songs of a Summer Night (Lynne's garden)* 1985.
Oil, wood on canvas, 165 x 222 cm. Purchased 1985.
Collection: Art Gallery of New South Wales.

Colin Lanceley (born 1938)

Colin Lanceley rejected the usual approach to Australian landscape painting as depicted in romantic bush paintings and focused his attention on the city and urban environment with which more of the population are familiar.

He moved away from conventional approaches to painting to more dynamic experiments with collage and assemblage of media. During the 1960s, Lanceley became increasingly interested in the litter of the consumer society and manipulated it to create works which pulsate with the energy of the city. The relationship of found objects is carefully considered as they are built up in 'layers of human activity'.

Gradually, Lanceley refined his work by introducing the shaped canvas, and responding to the local environment with an exciting use of brilliant colour. In *Songs of a Summer Night (Lynne's Garden)*, the artist has created a sensual experience of a garden at night.

Questions

1. How has the artist integrated the found objects with the flat areas of the painting?

2. With your finger, trace a pathway through the painting following the direction the lines and shapes lead. Stop momentarily on your journey and consider which sections of the work are real objects and which are flat painted areas.

40

MICHAEL JOHNSON, *Buji* 1986.
Oil on linen. The Robert Holmes à Court Collection.

Michael Johnson (born 1938)

Michael Johnson's paintings have developed from hard-edged abstract works with flat areas of colour in the 1960s and 1970s, to more expressive painterly works in the 1980s.

The painted surface of his most recent large-scale works is built up progressively in layers of oil paint. Each successive layer is applied by manipulating media in a variety of different ways ranging from a soft ground colour to broad thick brushstrokes and paint built up and smeared with a palette knife. The final layer of paint is squeezed straight from the tube to create a dynamic network of thickly encrusted, expressive lines. The vitality of the surface of these paintings is enhanced by the striking combination of vivid colours.

Albert Tucker (born 1914)

In the 1940s, Tucker's paintings were his personal response to the horrors of war and the 'moral decay' that pervaded society during wartime. The images were powerful and aggressive, and unacceptable to the art critics and the public at the time. The ferocity of the criticism prompted Tucker to leave Australia for England and Europe. Many Australian painters travelled abroad to study the works of other painters. They discovered that painters in Europe and the United States were working with a wide range of new and exciting materials. Tucker developed a technique of mixing synthetic emulsions with sand and gravel to build up his images on the canvas. The subject matter of his paintings consists of strange surrealist figures within the harsh arid Australian outback landscape. The imagery, brushwork and colours are bold, aggressive and expressive.

Albert Tucker stresses the importance of the artist working from his direct experience of life. Tucker's paintings depict strong, aggressive images of the Australian character moulded against the harsh environment. He works on time-ravaged faces depicting personalities he has experienced. The face takes on landscape proportions, creating a map of life's experiences. The personality of the subject is captured in all its different moods in several paintings of the one subject. *Antipodean Head* is part of a series. Texture is used to express the weathering and scarring of nature over a period of time. The surface quality of *Antipodean Head* is bonded with the meaning of the work.

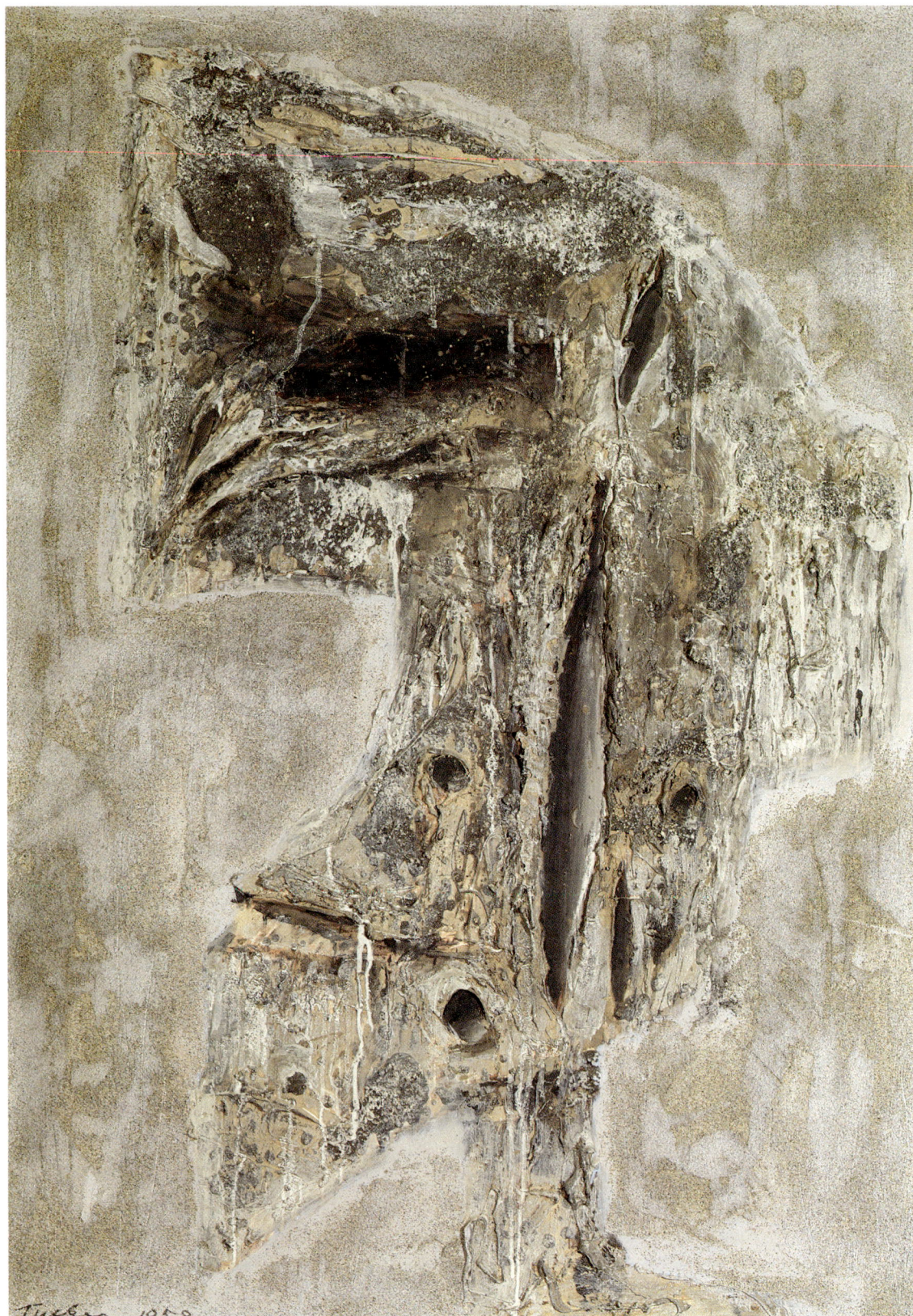

ALBERT TUCKER, *Antipodean Head* 1958.
Synthetic polymer paint and sand on composition board, 124.5 x 89.5 cm.
Collection: Australian National Gallery, Canberra.

Many sculptors select particular materials to work with because of their unusual surface qualities.

Bert Flugelman (born 1923)

Flugelman creates works in highly polished stainless steel. His forms are regular geometrical solids on a monumental scale. The highly polished surfaces reflect the images and light of the surrounding environment. *Cones* is situated in the sculpture garden of the Australian National Gallery.

HERBERT FLUGELMAN, *Cones* 1976-1982.
Stainless Steel.
Collection: Australian National Gallery, Canberra.

Questions

1 How would you describe the **scale** of this work?

2 How do the forms work in relation to the surrounding environment?

3 How does the texture of the surface of the forms compare/contrast with the surrounding textures?

César (born 1921)

César's early sculptures were created in stone and wood, however his love of metal soon led him to work almost exclusively in that material. Metal – iron, lead sheets, scrap metal, springs, iron, metal cans, bolts and used car bodies became the inspiration of César's sculptures. The unique surface textures of corroded and decayed metal led to both figurative and abstract sculptures.

During the early 1950s, sections of scrap metal were fused to create inventive, fantastic and grotesque animals. These became known as **ready-mades plus.** This period of César's sculpture was called the Amalgam Period. After 1955 César expressed himself on a monumental scale with solid structural sculptures made from iron plates. Often these welded sculptures were assemblages of compressed parts. This period became known as the Iron Plate period.

CESAR, *Petite Tete de Radiateur.*
Iron. Galerie Claude Bernard, Paris.

43

Ruby Brilliant (born 1946)

Ruby Brilliant explores surface quality in her art works and experiments with the creative possibilities of thread through knitting. She is concerned with visual symbols of her life experiences, translating them with fibre. Rich layers of colours and patterns result in images of cats, letters, memories, landscapes and dreams.

The knitted garment takes on a new identity. The garment becomes an art object to be hung or exhibited on the body. The knitted art work communicates with the viewer in the same way as a painting or sculpture. Ruby calls her knits 'mollages' – collages of mixed materials.

The development of the knit is somewhat spontaneous, with Ruby reacting intuitively to certain materials as she uses them. Although she uses traditional knitting stitches, Ruby manipulates these to create a highly original result. The symmetry and ordered patterns of traditional knitting are not used, instead more imaginative expressive compositions appear. The quality of the knitted surface is linked to the artist's experiments with paint – the brushstrokes, drips and splashes. Shape, colour, pattern and contrast – elements important to painting are important in the knitted works. Their tactile quality invites attention and proves what can be achieved when the artist goes beyond the boundaries of tradition or convention.

RUBY BRILLIANT, *Ghost Gums.*
Knitted cardigan.

RUBY BRILLIANT, *Hassan & Banjo* 1984.
Knitted jumper.

Texture Exercises

Texture guessing

1 Collect objects, natural or man-made, that have interesting textures, for example cones, shells, bark, wood or materials such as silk, fur, wool, hessian, etc.

2 In pairs, play a texture guessing game by putting an object or piece of something in a paper bag or box. Close your eyes and try to guess what the object is by how it feels to touch. Try to draw what you think it looks like by simply feeling it.

Texture rubbings

1 Go out into the playground, find surfaces that have an interesting texture or pattern, eg, concrete, wooden paling fences, grates on drains, brickwork, tyre treads, vents, louvres, signs on doors, wire mesh, number plates.

2 Place paper on the surface and rub over it with a soft pencil or wax crayon until the texture pattern appears on the paper. Do at least six different rubbings. Cut out and stick in your sketch book.

Simulated texture

Evaluate the rubbings you have made. Try to recreate the pattern created in each rubbing using a fine-pointed texta or pen using only lines.

Manipulating clay

1 Collect a variety of tools, implements and found objects, eg garlic press, toothpicks, mechanical parts such as nuts, bolts and cogs, twigs, keys, toothbrush, etc. You are going to use these to create different textures on a clay surface.

2 Roll out clay into an even slab. Cut out six clay squares (tiles). Using the tools you have collected, experiment with creating a variety of textures on the surface of the tiles.

3 Put aside to dry and fire. After bisque firing, experiment with different oxides and glazes. Try to emphasise the textures by rubbing back the glaze or oxide on the raised surfaces.

Relief ceramic landscape

1 Roll out a large clay slab. Using another slab, cut clay out into simple plant shapes and join to the original clay surface to create a landscape. Experiment with building up different levels. Using different tools, create a variety of textures on the shapes.

2 Allow to dry and bisque fire. Then glaze in either bright glazes (eg underglazes or onglazes) or natural earth glazes.

Animal forms in clay

1 Make two small pinch pots — join together and use this form as the basic body or head shape of an animal, or bird. It can be an imaginary creature. Add extra clay to create features such as arms and legs. Your teacher will help you with proper joining techniques.

2 Texture the surface of the form to create the pattern/texture of your animal.

Lino print

1 Explore the gardens and courtyards of the school. Find a place where plants stand in front of man-made structures. Notice the differences of shape and texture.

2 Make a simple drawing of the plant(s) in front of part of a building or man-made structure from a close point of view.

3 From this drawing create a design in which the natural textures or surface patterns and organic shapes of the plants contrast with the man-made textures and structures. Emphasise the line and pattern you see. This could be either a black and white print (one colour) or a print using three colours or more.

Experiment with a palette knife

1 Experiment with a palette knife and thick paint. How many different ways can you apply the paint to a thick surface such as cardboard using the palette knife?

2 Try to create a face using only the palette knife. Look closely at another student's face or your own face in a mirror. Which directions and angles dominate? Where can you detect edges? Follow the contours of the bone struc-

ture of your face with your hands and transfer this information to your painting.

Imaginary landscape/fantasy painting

1 Create a textured surface on heavy cardboard or canvas by experimenting with tissue paper soaked in Aquadhere (wood and paper glue) and/or plaster-impregnated gauze bandage (mod-rock) to build up interesting variations. Allow to dry rock-hard.

2 Consider the result. Use your imagination to visualise forms and textured images within the surface. Now use paint to enhance and clarify these forms to create a landscape or fantasy painting.

Weaving with mixed media

1 Collect a variety of material suitable for weaving. Try to choose some non-traditional materials (other than cotton and wool), such as old cassette tape, plastic tubing, cane reed, strips of hand-made paper, strips of material cut from old clothing, wire, cotton waste, feathers, straw, string, rope, raffia, strips of synthetic materials such as rayon and lurex.

2 Set up a frame (an old painting stretcher works well) with a series of evenly spaced nails on two opposite sides. Attach lengths of string in paràllel lines between opposite nails. This is called the **warp** and will support the materials you weave through it, which are called the **weft.**

3 Experiment with different combinations of your found materials to create a weaving which explores different possibilities of textured surfaces.

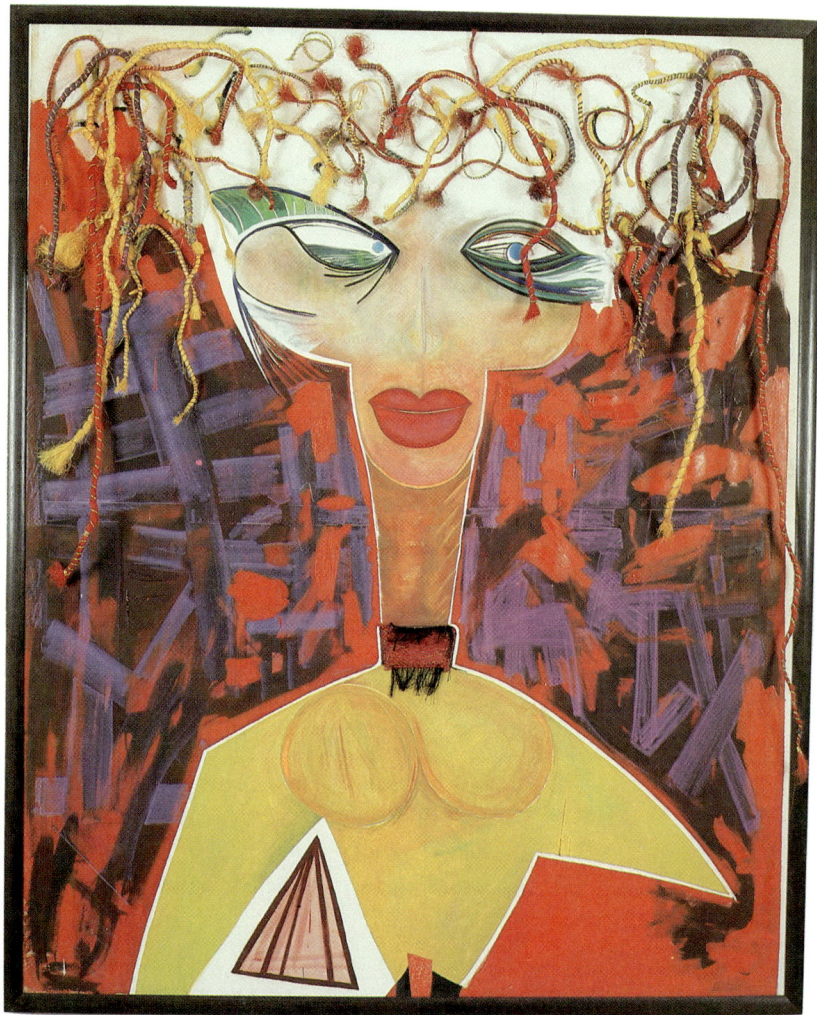

GABRIEL ROSATI, *Mona* 1987.
Mixed media. Collection of the artist.

Colour

Colour is an important part of the world we live in. Without colour we would see the world in shades of grey, white and black. Colour affects the way we feel. Some colours give us a warm, active, happy feeling (yellow, orange, red). These colours remind us of the sunshine and the heat of a glowing fire. Other colours create a cool, peaceful feeling (blue, green). These colours remind us of cool fresh water and shady trees.

Sometimes colour is used symbolically. In traffic lights, green indicates go ahead, all is clear, and red says, 'stop', danger! Blood is also red. A splash of red on a painting could suggest violence and spilt blood.

All colours are made from three **primary** colours.

When you mix two primary colours together you produce a **secondary** colour.

Red + yellow = orange   Yellow + blue = green   Blue + red = purple

If you mix together three primary colours in different quantities you create **tertiary** colours.

Tan   Brown   Khaki green

Exercises

1 Draw up a colour wheel like the one below and practise mixing colours in paint.

2 Try mixing some tertiary colours. If you mix colours that are opposite on the colour wheel you will create tertiary colours.
Orange + blue = ?
Yellow + purple = ?
Red + green = ?

If you add black to any colour you make a dark **tone** of that colour. This is called a **shade**. If you add white to a colour you will make a light tone of that colour. This is called a **tint**.

ROY DE MAISTRE, *Arrested Phrase from Beethoven's Ninth Symphony in Red Major* 1919-1935.
Oil on paperboard, 72.4 x 99 cm. Collection: Australian National Gallery, Canberra.

Roy De Maistre (1894-1968)

De Maistre drew on his study of music, and on inspiration from European Cubist and abstract art to create the earliest Australian abstract paintings. He translated musical scales into colour scales in such works as *Arrested Phrase from Beethoven's Ninth Symphony in Red Major*.

Questions

1 Look at the painting. Warm colours remind us of heat, the sun and fire.
List the colours in this painting which you think are warm.

2 Cool colours remind us of cool water and shady forests. List the colours which are cool.

3 Can you identify which parts of this painting appear to jump towards you? Which appear to recede? Explain why.

4 Look for the tints and shades in this painting. Which appear to come forward and which appear to be receding?

Grace Cossington Smith (1892-1984)

Grace Cossington Smith's approach to painting is somewhat similar to the work of the French Impressionists. An example hanging in the Art Gallery of New South Wales by Camille Pissarro (1830-1903) is called *Peasants' houses, Eragny* (1887). In this painting, Pissarro has used small dabs of pure colours placed side by side which are then blended by the viewer's eye from a distant viewpoint.

Grace Cossington Smith painted subjects from her immediate environment and infused a new life into what were considered everyday subject matters. Early in her career, Grace would go on regular trips to the city in Sydney to shop, see exhibitions and draw the busy streets. From her direct observations she captured the excitement of city life.

'I used to go out and sketch, make a drawing, not a very detailed one but just with the forms and I'd put a little note as to the colour. Then I'd come home and paint it in my studio'.

On one of these trips to the city Grace discovered the 'Lacquer Room' a city tearoom whose interior was designed by artist Thea Proctor. Grace was immediately attracted by the brilliant colour of the scarlet and green furniture. She quickly sketched the scene complete with the individual facial expressions of the customers as they gazed straight out towards the artist. Grace rejected traditional perspective with every form in the room organised on a flat plane. The darker figures contrast with the lighter colours of the background and the bold forms of the red chairs. Grace Cossington Smith was one of the earliest Australian artists to be influenced by the European post-Impressionist movement.

Grace had a special love of the Australian bush. In the 1930s, motoring trips to the country enabled her to work directly from the landscape. Her strong technique captured the light and mystical colour of the bush. Broken brushstrokes were carefully built up side by side as an arrangement of squares never to be reworked. The Australian bush was one of her most challenging subjects.

In her later life, Grace found her more immediate environment more accessible than the bush and focused on her home for inspiration; her bedroom, belongings – sewing machine, wardrobe, simple items of furniture, and views through windows and open doors. She was attracted to the brilliant sunlight which illuminated her room. Even the areas of shadow are painted with pure cool colours which shimmer with energy, while sunlight bounces off reflecting surfaces. Inanimate objects are respected as much as people and landscape. The furniture is given a life of its own. What would usually be a cluttered everyday scene has a new beauty as the forms relate to each other and the viewer.

Grace Cossington Smith's contribution to Australian art must be considered both from her direct technique and her inspiring transformation of everyday subject matter.

'All forms of landscape, interior, still-life, flowers, animals, people have inarticulate grace and beauty. Painting to me is expressing this form in colour vibrant with light but containing this other sunlit quality which is unconscious and belongs to all things created. Art is the expression of all things that are lovely. Expressing things unseen, the golden thread running through time.'

GRACE COSSINGTON SMITH, *Interior with Wardrobe Mirror* 1955.
Oil on canvas, 91.5 x 73.7 cm. Purchased 1967.
Collection: Art Gallery of New South Wales.

CAMILLE PISSARRO, *Peasants' Houses, Eragny* 1887.
Oil on canvas, 59 x 71.1 cm. Purchased 1935.
Collection: Art Gallery of New South Wales.

Questions

1 Look at the painting *Interior with Wardrobe Mirror*. How has the artist created the effect of shadow? What colours are used?

2 How has the artist created the illusion of depth in the room using tonal variations of colours? This may be more apparent in some areas of the painting than others.

3 How has the paint been applied to the canvas? What optical effect does this create? Are there any areas of one flat colour? Compare this painting with Matisse's *The Purple Robe* on page 53.

Henri Matisse (1869-1954)

The **space** in Matisse's paintings is flattened – there appears to be no depth in this room. The flowers and clothing are painted in flat, unmodulated colours. This is emphasised by the continuation of the patterned surface of the floor up onto the robe and the wall surface. The figure has no modelling – it is defined only by flat colours outlined in heavy black lines. The forms are simplified. Matisse created a new concept of pictorial space through colour and line.

Matisse was considered the leader of the Fauve movement in the early 1900s. He pursued the same philosophy to art throughout his career. 'Les Fauves' means wild beasts – it was a derogatory term used by the art critics of the time to describe their unconventional, wildly unrestrained colouristic paintings. Their aim was the emotional use of colour rather than representation of naturalistic colour.

Matisse was influenced by Manet, Gauguin, Oriental art and Islamic art. Colour, line and space became the essential elements of his decorative compositions. He avoided modelling his forms, preferring to use flat areas of rich pure colour applied with strong, bold brushwork.

Rather than suggesting symbolic meanings, Matisse's paintings are meant to be enjoyed purely for their decorative quality. He painted a wide range of subject matter ranging from organised still lifes, interiors and portraits set in his studio, to exotic landscapes inspired by his experiences of Morocco and Spain.

In his interiors, such as the *Purple Robe* decorative motifs were introduced to create a variety of richly patterned surfaces. The combination of sensuous line and vivid colour flowing across the picture surface creates a joyous playful mood.

Questions

1   Why do you think Matisse called this painting the *Purple Robe*? Does the robe dominate the painting?

2.   Matisse has divided this painting into several areas of flat colour. How many of these areas can you see?

3.   Locate areas of colour and pattern within the painting that contrast with each other.

4.   What aspects or parts of the painting give you a feeling of spatial depth or perspective?

5.   What makes the figure of the woman stand out from the background of this painting?

6.   Matisse often distorted and simplified objects for the sake of the total painting. How does the woman's face differ from other paintings of women you have seen?

7.   Could this painting be considered a portrait or a still-life composition? Why?

8.   Matisse has used a variety of linework in this painting. On a sheet of drawing paper sketch the different types of lines you can see.

9.   The lines Matisse has used could be described as rhythmic. Trace the pathway your eye follows through the painting. What is meant by the term rhythmic?

10.   Do the colours of this painting stir any particular emotions in you? If so what are they and why do they do this? Do any other elements in the painting create or emphasise this feeling?

11.   Matisse was influenced by Eastern art. Research examples of Persian carpets and oriental paintings. Draw the types of lines evident in these examples. Compare these with those painted by Matisse.

12.   Look through this book or other art books you have access to and locate works which you think may have been influenced by Matisse's innovations. What similarities do they have?

HENRY MATISSE, *Purple Robe and Anemones* 1937. (opposite)
Oil on canvas, 73.1 x 60.3 cm.
The Cone Collection, formed by Dr Claribel Cone and Miss Etta Cone of Baltimore, Maryland.
Baltimore Museum of Art, BMA 1950.261.
©Succession H. Matisse
DACS 1991

Mark Rothko (1903-1970)

By filling the entire canvas with colour, Rothko evokes a sense of calm. These paintings became colour environments which directly involve the viewer. They became known as colourfield paintings.

Rothko developed a technique of staining the paint on to the canvas, to build up colours in veils adding to their intensity. These hazy areas of colour seem to hover on the surface of the painting, suspended in front of the viewer. To some extent, the veils of colour appear to advance and envelop the viewer; leaving the confines of the picture plane and crossing between that area of space, into the viewer's space.

These seemingly simple, undetailed surfaces have a powerful physical and psychological effect on the viewer. Rothko uses subtle variations of colours, often in warm and cool combinations eg, *Orange and Yellow* (1956) and *White and Greens in Blue* (1957). The boundaries between each colour area are undefined and appear to be constantly shifting. The key elements in Rothko's colourfield paintings are colour and size. The huge scale of the works reinforcing the physical and emotional impact on the spectator.

MARK ROTHKO, Untitled (Red) 1958.
Oil on canvas, 208.4 x 124.5 cm. Purchased through the Art Foundation of Victoria 1982.
National Gallery of Victoria.

Questions

1 Allow yourself to experience this painting for a period of one or two minutes. How do the colours used make you feel? How many colours can you see?

2 Is there a dominant colour area?

3 What else attracts your attention? Why?

4 Are there any forms or edges in the painting?

5 Is there any suggestion of movement?

6 Imagine you were confronted by a similar work by Rothko painted in shades of black and dark blue. What mood or feeling would this evoke?

Bridget Riley (born 1931)

Bridget Riley works with unusual colour combinations creating optical sensations. Her inspiration came from her sensitivity to the optical effects of changing light on natural forms. Riley's paintings are non-representational and are made up of coloured bands or waves which seem to advance and recede, vibrating on the surface.

The viewer experiences the interaction of one colour with another as they appear in carefully organised groupings. The artist has used a wide range of colour combinations including early compositions – black, white and grey paintings in which she has experimented with spatial qualities and visual contrasts. These works predominated in the 1960s, pure colours were gradually introduced during the 1970s and by the 1980s, more intense colours were introduced.

Bridget Riley organises the work's development from experimenting with colour relationships, investigating reactions to colours, mixing exact colour, preparing small scale cartoons of the finished composition, to finally directing teams of painters to create the finished work.

The artist selects titles for her works which clarify their intent, the mood the artist is hoping to create eg, *Shiver* (1964), *Static* (1966) and *Zing* (1971).

The paintings create a powerful sensation through their huge scale and repetitive rhythm. When the viewer is confronted with these colour environments a feeling of involvement with the energy of the work is generated.

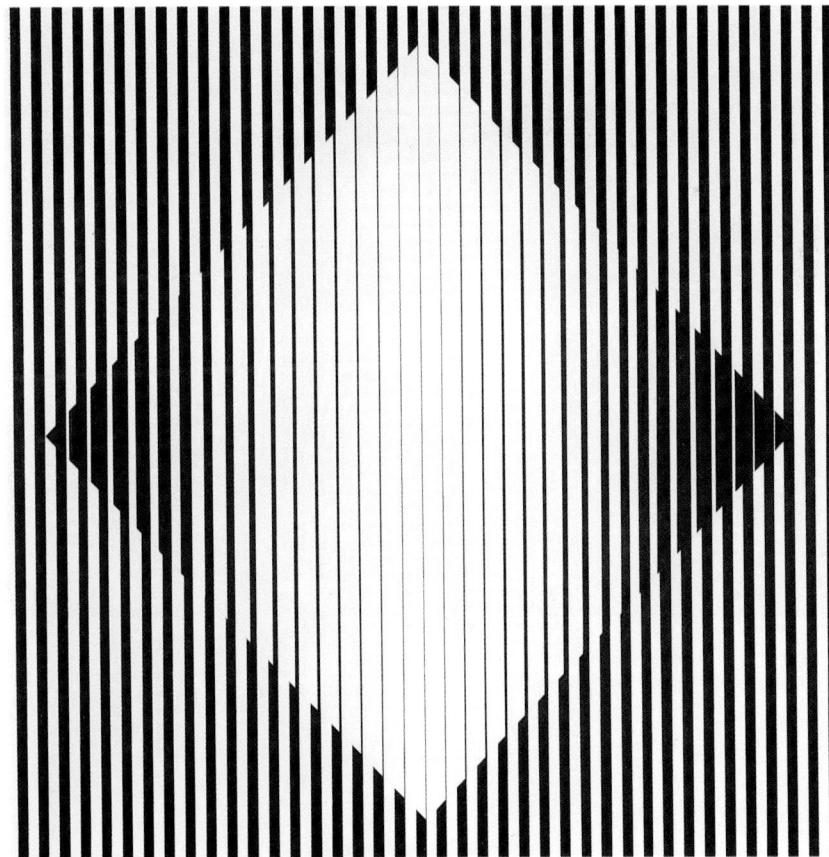

BRIDGET RILEY, *Opening* 1961.
Tempera on hardboard, 101.9 x 101.6 cm.
Felton Bequest 1967. National Gallery of Victoria.

Alun Leach-Jones (born 1937)

Alun Leach-Jones creates large scale abstract compositions which exude energy. Vibrant colours are interwoven in a complex structure of lines and shapes. These designs are formulated with great care, by a process of planning working drawings on a smaller scale, then transferring these on to canvas.

The artist has control over the careful selection of every shape and colour, often choosing primary and secondary colours because of their bold impact. Black is used in his recent works, resulting in a more mysterious mood. White outlines emphasise the sharp clarity of the shapes, so that they seem to break free of the picture space.

The viewer feels an immediate relationship with the works; their energy simultaneously reaches out and draws the viewer in. The dynamic quality of Alun Leach-Jones' paintings is achieved by exacting selection of colours and knowledge of their relationships with each other. The projection of lines and shapes twisting and turning in every direction adds to this sensation of forceful movement.

Alun Leach-Jones has been called a Geometric Abstractionist, a term applied to artists who create carefully planned compositions of abstract shapes, where colour is permitted to become the subject.

ALUN LEACH-JONES, *Romance of Death No. 9* 1984.
Acrylic on canvas, 172 x 350 cm. Collection: Perth Cultural Centre.

ALUN LEACH-JONES at work in the Fremantle Arts Centre Studio, August 1987.

Andy Warhol (1928-1988)

After a background in commercial art, Andy Warhol exposes the public to imagery from their daily experience. He deals with the stereotype image and markets it as an art product. Warhol explores concepts such as fame, death, disaster, violence, money and power; controlling our reactions to them. Mass production enters fine arts with Warhol's introduction of the technique of using photographic enlargements silk-screened on to canvas.

Crude, synthetic colour was silk screened onto canvas to create an art work untouched by human hands. Horrific images taken from the news media were given repeated exposure by Warhol, depersonalising the event. The only irregularities in these repeated images are created by the texture of the paint and the intensity of the colours. Our attention is diverted away from the real horrors depicted, to the coloured surface and we become desensitised.

Warhol uses colour in a highly expressive way. His choices range from sinister monochrome orange washes to subtle colour harmonies. The artist was extremely concerned with the testing and selection process of each colour to create the desired emotional and physical effect. The broad areas of colour employed were chosen to express the **moral and aesthetic blankness** that Warhol saw in the period.

ANDY WARHOL, *Orange Disaster # 5* 1963.
Acrylic and silkscreen enamel on canvas, 269.2 x 207.6 cm.
Gift of Harry N Abrams Family Collection.
Photograph: David Heald. Collection: Solomon R Guggenheim Museum, New York.

DAVID VAN NUNEN, *Heliotropical Rainforest: Wingham* 1983.
Oil on linen, 200 x 190 cm. Collection of the artist.

David van Nunen (born 1952)

Australian artist, David van Nunen uses the Australian landscape as his inspiration. Rainforests, other plant forms and the foreshores of Sydney Harbour are expressed as areas of strong colour and bold linework.

The lush vegetation of the rainforest is a recurrent theme in van Nunen's work, influenced by his early childhood in Queensland and the north coast of New South Wales. *Heliotropical Rainforest: Wingham,* represents a remembered experience of three days camping at Wingham outside Taree and further direct investigation of the Palm Grove in the Sydney Botanic Gardens.

In this painting, van Nunen captures the brilliance of the Australian light at midday. Bright cadmium yellow and white are used to suggest glare and passages of water. Complementary colours such as violets and yellows, reds and greens extend in many directions, overlapping and interlocking to create a complex structure of bold patterns. The angles and jarring geometric lines build up energy which pulsates within a confined space.

Rather than conforming to European trends in painting in which he feels aggression and foreboding gloom predominate, van Nunen sees his work as being a celebration of sight and space. In his dazzling compositions he captures the life force of the natural environment. He sees himself as an urban person making a serious statement about the beauty of the threatened Australian rainforest.

'I have always experienced a strong sense of place, and my paintings are emblematic evocations of the Australian landscape, conveying its intense light and vivid local colour.'

DAVID VAN NUNEN, *Camp Cove* 1987.
Oil on linen, 152.5 x 183 cm. Collection of John Antico.

Colour Exercises

Choosing a colour scheme for design

When you are ready to start painting a design, you must make some decisions about the colours you will use.

1 What mood are you trying to create?
Certain colours create particular moods, feelings and atmosphere.
- A warm sunny mood? Try using reds, oranges, yellows.
- A natural, fresh atmosphere? Try blues, greens.
- A mood of uncertainty, mystery? Try purples with red, blue.
- A cold, sinister mood? Try greys with blues.

2 A good starting point is a **colour harmony** (colours that are similar – near each other on the colour wheel). These are colour harmonies.

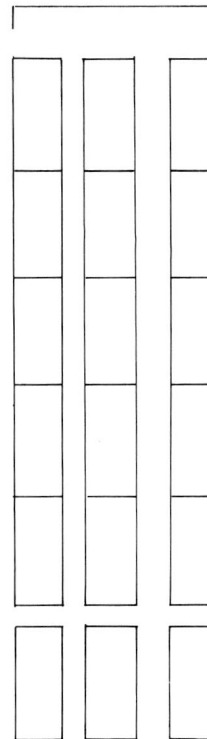

yellow	red	blue
orange	purple	green
red	blue	yellow
blue	yellow	red

3 A **contrasting** colour is opposite on the colour wheel. A colour harmony plus one contrasting colour can create an interesting colour scheme for a design. Of course all these colours can be mixed with black or white (neutrals) to create darker and lighter tones of each colour.

4 Choose a colour scheme according to what mood you are aiming to create. Rule up a tone grid in your sketchbook (or on paper) to experiment with the colours you have chosen.

Colour harmony | Contrast

add white (two tones)

pure colour

add black (two tones)

add grey

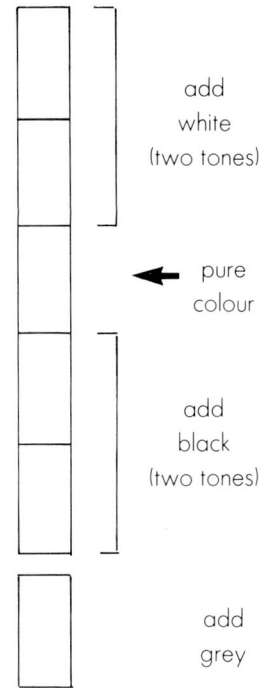

5 Paint the pure colour in the middle box. Add white to the colour to create two lighter tones. Add black to the colour to create two darker tones. Add a little white and black to create a duller tone.

Pattern painting

1 Put out a large and a small brush, paint, water, and four small pieces of art paper. You are going to experiment with colours by creating patterns with paint. You are to cover the entire surface of each page with patterns – try not to leave any white space.

2 Apply the paint to the surface in various ways, such as dabs, spots, twirls and lines. Use different types of lines. See how colours react next to each other. Can you create a feeling of peace and tranquility? A violent mood? A happy mood?

3 Evaluate your patterns as you go. What sort of lines, shapes and colours have you used?

Letter design

1 Using the capital letters of your name create a design in which the letter shapes are **repeated.** Vary the **size** and **direction** of the shapes. Overlap some shapes and make sure there is a **balance** of shapes throughout the design.

2 Paint the completed design in **complementary** colours (opposite on the colour wheel).

Creating a colour environment with collage or photo-montage

1 Select a colour for your environment.

2 Collect images and objects only in your chosen colour. Manipulate these images and objects to create an abstract composition. Fill the entire picture space of the paper with images and objects in your colour.

Creating a painted colour environment

1 Select the colour of your environment.

2 Choose a variety of painting implements, eg palette knife, fine brush, fitch brush, spray gun or spray can, felt pen, biro, crayon, pastel.

3 Apply your colour to the canvas by manipulating application techniques using a variety of implements.

4 Consider the different tonal qualities of the colour and textural qualities of the medium.

Aboriginal Art

1 Consider some of the Aboriginal art you have already studied. On a small sheet of art paper, create a design based on animal forms.

2 Using earthy colours paint this design. Tertiary colours are earthy colours. Refer to your colour experiments for mixing these colours.

3 When the paint is dry, use a fine-point texta to outline each section and then work over most of the spaces with patterns of lines (straight and wavy) and dots in lines.

Product Design

1 Investigate colours used in packaging. Visit the local supermarket and look at the variety of different products displayed on the shelves.
Do you notice any similarities in packaging of the same type of product? (For example, cereals or washing products).

2 List the colours used in the different types of products. How is the packaging design of foodstuffs different to other products such as household cleaners?

3 Do a careful reproduction of one of these packages.

4 Design your own package to compete with a product of your choice.

Art room composition

1 Explore your art room for interesting objects — arrange them on an art table.

2 Create a composition first in pencil using the objects on a table and a view of the art room. Work over the drawing reconsidering the type of lines you used. What mood are you creating? What sort of lines should you use to create a particular mood? What sort of mood do curved lines create compared with angular straight lines?

3 Simplify forms, emphasise the linear quality of objects. Now paint your composition. Be careful to choose colours that reflect or emphasise the mood you are trying to create.

Extension activity

Explore the school gardens and courtyards — find areas of wild plant growth and interesting shapes and lines. Create a small painting called *The Rhythm of Life* — the emphasis should be on **colour** and **line.**

Contrast

Contrast can describe differences in shape or form.

Artists often emphasise different qualities in their art works. When viewed together, the differences between objects become more obvious. When objects or elements of design have noticeably different qualities we call this **contrast**. The success of many artists' works relies on the viewer recognising obvious contrasts.

Claes Oldenburg (born 1929)

The Pop Art sculptor, Claes Oldenburg, has taken familiar objects from the urban environment and everyday life. He has created sculptures which stimulate our imagination through obvious contrasts with reality. The artist has manipulated scale to create sculptures which contrast in size with the real object.

An everyday object such as a toilet seat acquires a new power when its form is reversed. The visual and tactile quality of the object is in sharp contrast with that of the real object.

Oldenburg introduces contradictions of the normal properties of the real world.

CLAES OLDENBURG, *Soft Toilet* 1966. (opposite)
Canvas filled with kapok, wood and metal pipes painted with liquitex.

Tonal values in a work of art may be in sharp contrast.

KEN REINHARD, *To the Big E* 1974.
Mixed media, 94.5 x 155.5 cm. Collection of Ron Hodgson.

Surface qualities or textures can be in contrast.

DALE JONES-EVANS, *Table* 1985.
Concrete, steel and glass. Biltmoderne, Victoria.

Dale Jones-Evans

New concepts in furniture design are being explored by some of Australia's furniture artists and designers. Many of these artists have utilised a variety of materials in their designs. These include plastic, glass, cement and metals.

This unique *Table* 1985 was designed with raw materials in mind. An architectural construction of planes that slice through one another.

Recent developments in furniture design raise aesthetic issues. The 'Nouveau Wave' of designers do not have any loyalty to traditional furniture design or materials such as wood. Qualities which are important in sculpture are equally important in *Table*. The designer shows great sensitivity to materials, surface quality and space. The *Table* is visually balanced without superfluous decoration. The table is a strong design both aesthetically and functionally. The designer has created a structurally sound piece of furniture with an economy of materials. The construction of the table is open, refined and sensitive to the physical properties of the materials. The interlocking forms are carefully placed with a kind of geometric precision highlighting the unique surface qualities of glass concrete and steel.

Contrast Exercises and Experiments

Exercises

1 Collect a selection of different surfaces or textures or photographs of these surfaces. Arrange in a grid to emphasise the contrasts between these surfaces.

ANGELA HOLMES, student.

2 Collect discarded materials suitable for assembling a junk sculpture. Experiment with organising the materials into interesting combinations which emphasise their obvious differences. The visual and tactile qualities of materials may provide the following possibilities for effective contrasts.

Possible contrasts

(a) heavy/light — feathers with wood, stone, cement, metal
(b) solid/transparent — perspex, stone, wood, metal, clay, glass, mirror
(c) thin/thick — wire, heavy rope, string, wood, paper, cane reed
(d) smooth/rough — wax, nails, corrugated iron, wire, barbed wire, wood, perspex, hessian, silk, stone, paper, cement
(e) natural/man-made — wax, plastic, wire, cane, glass, rubber.

Further contrasts

Large/small, dark/light, curved/angular, moving/inert, saggy/rigid, soft/hard.

Harmony

Harmony can be described as an agreeable arrangement of the elements of design. When we view a harmonious arrangement of elements it creates a pleasant response in the viewer. The repetition of the same visual element in a composition can create a harmonious relationship.

Curves and flowing lines derived from circular organic forms dominate this composition and create a pleasing rhythm resulting in a feeling of harmony.

Exercises

1 List and sketch examples of harmonious forms in your school and local environment. Transfer the information from these sketches to create a harmonious composition suitable for creating a repeat pattern.

2 Plan your design so that it is **harmonious** with the shape it is contained within.

ROGER KEMP, *Archetype* 1981.
Synthetic polymer paint on canvas, 214 x 473 cm. Purchased 1985.
Collection: Art Gallery of New South Wales.

Focal Point

Many art works have an area of interest to which the eye is directed or focused. This is called a **focal point.** The focal point can be created in many different ways.

1 Contrasting shapes/forms or colours.
2 Isolating forms from surrounding ones.
3 Directional lines to lead the eye.
4 Placement of forms centrally.
5 Pattern or detail to highlight areas.
6 Contrast of size to focus attention.

However, not all artworks have a focal point. Many designs have an overall repetitive pattern such as dress fabric or curtain material.

In *Armoured Faun Attacked by Parrots,* our attention is focused on the strange skeletal figure that vaguely resembles the dead trees in the background, because of its central placement.

The **directional lines** created by the parrots wings as well as their bright colours further reinforces the focus towards the central figure.

ALBERT TUCKER, *Armoured Faun Attacked by Parrots* 1969.
Synthetic polymer paint, tempera on composition board, 152.2 x 122 cm.
Collection: Australian National Gallery, Canberra.

Questions

1 What do you imagine this strange creature is? Is it living?

2 Why do the parrots seem to want to hang around it?

3 Why do you think all the trees are dead?

4 Where do you think this scene is? Is it part of the real world?

RICHARD LARTER, *Cal-jo Shift* 1970.
Synthetic polymer paint and glitter on composition board, 122.2 x 183 cm.
Collection: Australian National Gallery, Canberra.

Richard Larter (born 1929)

In *Cal-Jo Shift*, Richard Larter has transformed an ugly city environment into the inspiration for an exciting art work. The direct experience of the city at night gave him a kaleidoscopic viewpoint of what is an unappealing and monotonous environment by day.

'I had been riding my motorbike after midnight down Parramatta Road in and out of Sydney – at speed at that time of night with very little traffic around, the place was a succession of flashing lights and reflections. At this time I had also filmed some of these journeys with the camera, punching out single frames, so that 10 miles flashed by in less than a minute on the screen. From these images I conceived the painting.'

The artist's subject matter is speed and light. Fragmented images of fast food stores and gaudy signs are a comment on the superficial and impersonal quality of city life.

This abstract painting, with its torn, irregular forms assembled in a collage-like manner has been described as a kind of *'futuristic-expressionism'*. To capture the irridescence of his chaotic subject matter, the artist has experimented freely with a variety of media and techniques.

'I used mini-rollers and acrylic paint. I rolled over glazes of PVA containing liquid pigments and encapsulating glitters and pearlescents. These were layered into the paintings then glazes of washes of transparent coloured PVA were added. Next I rolled out striped colours, then the brushwork and finally a very thick varnish of PVA for permanence.'

The area of bright red paint towards the centre left of the painting *Cal-jo Shift* focuses our attention for two reasons:

- it has very little pattern on its surface, in contrast to the surrounding highly patterned and textured areas
- the warm tones of red appear to jump forward from the picture plane while the cooler bluish, grey/browns and purples recede.

Questions

1 How many different sorts of areas of pattern or texture can you find in this work?

2 How often is each pattern repeated throughout the painting?

3 What colour seems to be repeated throughout, holding the painting together as a unified whole?

Charles Blackman (born 1928)

Charles Blackman is a figurative painter who interprets people in their urban environment in an expressive and symbolic way. His paintings are largely autobiographical, influenced by his working class background and his relationships with his wife (who is blind) and his child.

The lonely isolated figure in *The Shadow* draws our attention away from the surrounding environment. The curvilinear forms of the human figure contrast markedly with the rectilinear forms of the building behind. The warm orange areas on the ground and the figure draw the eye forward away from the cool bluish/purple hues of the buildings.

CHARLES BLACKMAN, *The Shadow* 1953.
Tempera on cardboard, 59 x 75 cm.
Collection: Heide Park and Art Gallery, Melbourne.

Vulnerable, lone figures reflect Blackman's sensitive preoccupation with relationships of people with one another. Isolation and alienation are common themes recurring in his work. The figures communicate more by their gesture than through their expressionless gazes. These works possess strange juxtapositions. The passive fragile mood of the paintings is at variance with Blackman's bold simplistic handling of paint and the scale of the works.

Realism and abstraction are allowed to co-exist in his compositions. Layers of clarity and obscurity are organised into two and three dimensional space.

Questions

1 Who do you imagine this figure to be?
2 What time of day is it?
3 Why is the figure alone? Why are there no other people in the painting?
4 Where do you think the figure is?
5 Why doesn't the figure show her face?

Clifton Pugh (born 1924)

Whether painting portraits or the Australian landscape, Clifton Pugh's work is an expressive reaction to his experiences. His compositions have an intrinsic abstract pattern which has been greatly influenced by his appreciation of Aboriginal art. His paintings have a fine balance between creative shapes without excessive distortion. Our eyes focus on particular objects within the composition often defined by bold energetic lines. The repetition of these lines creates a dynamic circular rhythm.

The circular contours of the parents' arms lead the eye from the face of the mother around to the encircled children and then back to the face of the mother completing a cycle. The lighter tones of the mother's and children's faces and clothing act to further hold our attention within this circular area.

Questions

1 Why do you think the figure of the father is painted in darker tones?
2 Who do you think the male figure is?
3 How does the form of the male figure fit into the total image?

CLIFTON PUGH, *The Muse and Ourselves.*
Oil on canvas. Collection: Australian National University, Canberra.

Focal Point Exercises

1 Develop an abstract design in which contrast of shapes, colours and size create a focal point in the design. Use what you have learnt about colour and shape in previous exercises.

2 Go for a walk out into the local area. Find an interesting view down a street. Sketch out a view that uses one point perspective to create a focus. Use coloured pencils, cray-pas, fine-point textas or other drawing materials to complete your drawing.

3 On a large sheet of art paper, draw a hallway in the school or in your home from a standing viewpoint, using one point perspective. Remember all vertical lines remain vertical. All horizontal lines above your eye-level appear to tilt upward, those on your eye level stay horizontal, and those below your eye level appear to tilt down. Notice where your vanishing point is. Now on another large sheet of art paper, draw the view from the other end of the hall looking back but now sit down or lie on the ground. Notice how the different vanishing point and eye level creates a totally different effect. Decide where the light source is in both views and paint the two drawings in different colour schemes. Try to create two different moods.

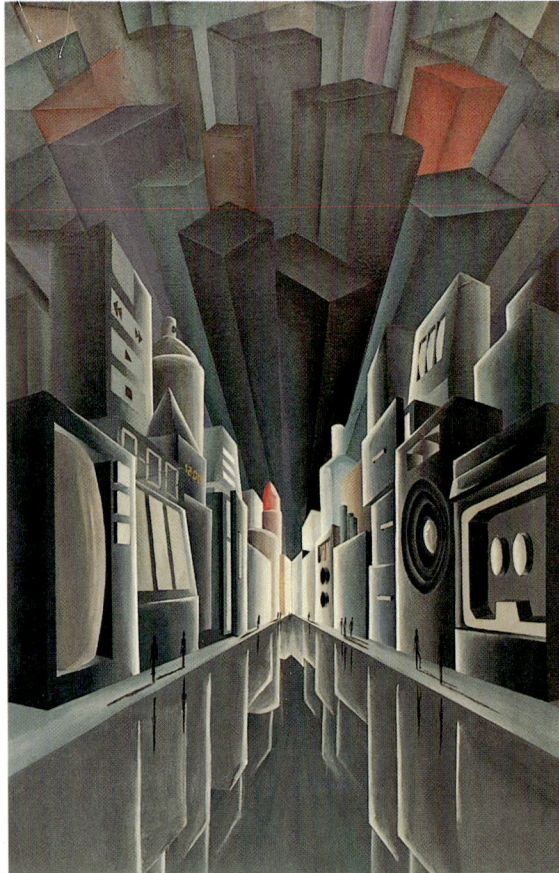

STEVEN CHUI, student.

The one-point perspective lines in the work *Technocratic Domain*, lead the eye through the painting past the monumental technology towards the horizon. From that point on the horizon, the directional lines of the cubic forms in the upper half of the painting surge upwards and forwards.

Questions

1 Does one particular image create a focal point in this painting? Why?

2 How is tonal variation used effectively in this work to focus attention?

3 Why, in your opinion, has the artist chosen the colours he has?

4 What role does man play in the society portrayed in this work?

5 What society do you think is being portrayed?

Space

The area in which we create a work of art is called **space**. Space is present in every work of art. The elements of design are arranged in space.

In art we can create two-dimensional space on a flat surface. This space is called the **picture space**. Picture space is used in drawing, painting and printmaking. Refer to the woodblock print *Fuchsia* by Margaret Preston, on page 74.

All the elements of the painting or print exist on the picture surface.

Artists can create the illusion of space being endless – infinite space. We experience infinite space in the natural environment. Perspective is a device used by artists to create this feeling. Refer to the painting *Sydney Harbour* by Arthur Streeton, on page 75.

The illusion of space on a flat surface can be created by several methods.

Scale and Size

By adjusting the size of objects, an artist can create a feeling of space.

Position

The artist's placement of the subject is important. The closer the image is positioned to the viewer's eye line, the further away it appears.

Overlapping

The object the artist places in front of another is generally considered to be closer to the viewer.

Detail

Artists can create a feeling of distance in the flat picture space by diminishing the detail. In this way objects further away do not appear as clearly.

Colour

Distance or depth can also be suggested by the placement of warm and cool colours (see section on colour). Artists use warm colours to advance objects towards the viewer. Cool colours are used to recede. Thus the object painted in a cool colour appears further away from us.

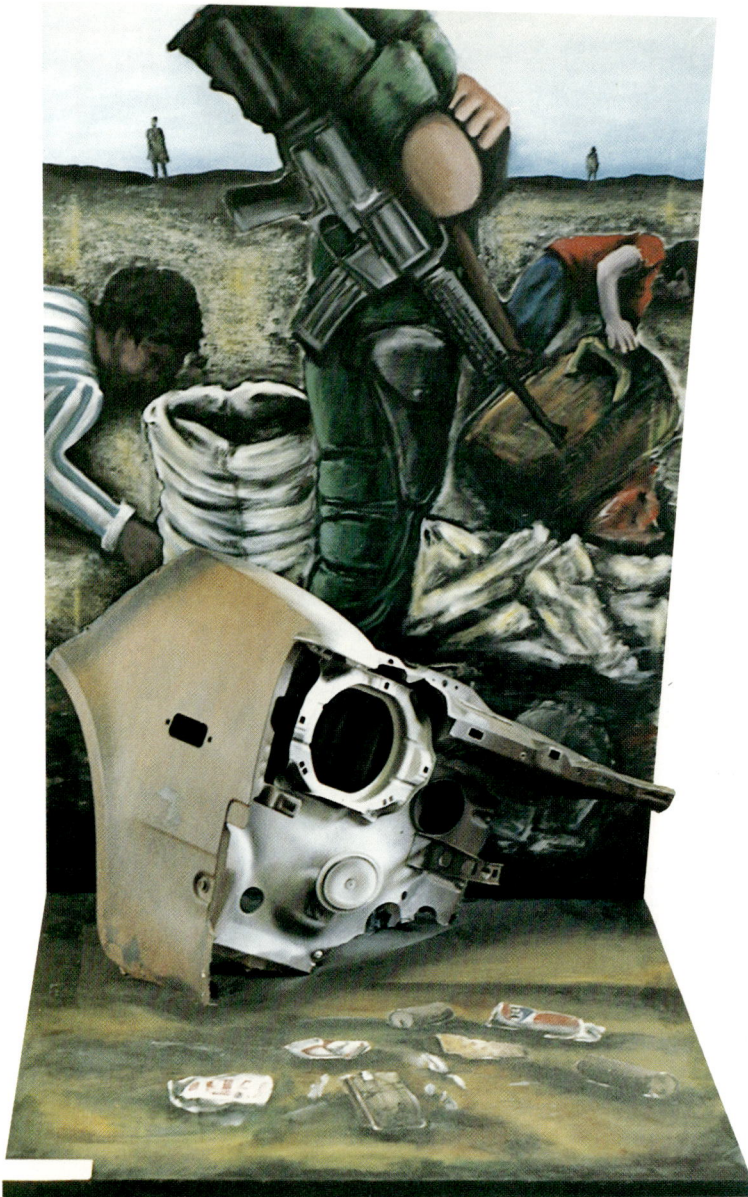

ANDREW JONES, student.

73

Margaret Preston (1875-1963)

Margaret Preston's art expresses a deep commitment to the true nature of the Australian environment through painting and printmaking. The Aboriginal artists' understanding and sensitivity to nature was a major influence on her work.

Woodblock printing became an artform at which she excelled. Influenced by Japanese prints, she developed her unique decorative designs. Still-life subjects harbour views and rural landscapes were depicted in striking contrasts of black and white, often being hand-coloured.

Preston was both highly original and prolific in her work, having produced over 400 prints during her lifetime.

MARGARET PRESTON, *Fuchsia* 1928.
Hand-coloured woodblock print on paper, 27.2 x 27 cm. Collection: Australian National Gallery.

Arthur Streeton (1867-1943)

Streeton was a member of a group of Australian painters called the Heidelberg School. Other artists in the group were Tom Roberts, Charles Conder, Julian Ashton and Frederick McCubbin. These artists were inspired by the *plein air* approach to painting of the French Impressionists. They set up art camps outside Melbourne, in Heidelberg painting outdoors, observing and recording their responses to the Australian bush from direct experience. The Heidelberg School painters were attempting to break away from the early Australian colonial style of landscape painting, more reminiscent of the English countryside. They developed a new and distinctive style of painting that was true to the Australian landscape.

Streeton manipulated paint with a brushwork technique very similar to the French Impressionists – and like the Impressionists he was interested in recording the effect of light heat and sun on the Australian landscape. Streeton captured the effect of the dazzling brilliance of the light in Australia by painting in a very high key.

ARTHUR STREETON, *Sydney Harbour.*
Oil on canvas, 120.6 x 120.6 cm. Felton Bequest 1910.
National Gallery of Victoria.

ALBERT GIACOMETTI, *City Square* 1948.
Bronze, 21.6 x 64.5 x 43.8 cm. Collection: The Museum of Modern Art, New York. Purchase.

In Art we may also use **negative space.** This is the space which exists around the objects in the painting or can be seen as a hole of light or air in a sculpture. Negative space is considered as important as positive form.

If both are considered properly we say that the work of art is balanced.

Giacometti's figurative sculptures such as *City Square*, suggest feelings of isolation, despair and anxiety. The sculptor has elongated the proportions of the figures to heighten their awkwardness and alienation from each other and the viewer. Although arranged in a group, the figures seem to follow separate pathways in their own space, creating a feeling of uncertainty. A timeless quality is achieved, with the figures petrified in their world.

Space can be real. This type of space is sometimes known as **plastic space.** We can experience three-dimensional objects in real space. Sculptures exist in real space.

MARIA KOZIC, *The Birds* 1981.
Plastic fishing line and stuffing, 365.8 x 426.7 cm. Courtesy of Roslyn Oxley 9 Gallery.

KEN UNSWORTH, Untitled 1975.
River stones, steel wires, 215 x 140 x 104.5 cm. Collection: Australian National Gallery, Canberra.

Exercises using space

View from a window

1 Look out the window of your classroom or your bedroom. You may see a distant view.
Using pencil, sketch the main images you see.

2 Experiment with creating a feeling of distance or infinite space by drawing images smaller as they appear further away.

3 Add greater visible detail to the objects closer to you with patterns and textures etc.

4 Extend the drawing into a painting by carefully selecting suitable colours. You may use realistic colours or choose a different colour scheme, however remember that warm colours advance and cool colours recede. Finally experiment with the intensity of the colours you have chosen. The further away an object is, the lighter or paler the colours appear. Objects seem to merge together with distance.

Pastel drawing of the art room

1 Find an interesting viewpoint of your art room. Include several pieces of furniture in the arrangement such as easels, stools, desks, perhaps the sink and window sill.

2 Do a large pencil drawing. Try to draw the objects as three-dimensional forms. Observe details such as size, position and overlapping shapes. Using pastels, try to create the effect of depth or distance. Select warm colours for those areas in strong light or close to you. Select cool colours for areas further away or areas of shadow. Experiment with blending the pastels to create interesting combinations of colours or new colours.

360° Panoramic View

1 As a class group select a location for your 360° class group drawing. Your teacher will allocate a number to each student. Seat yourselves in a circle facing outwards. Each student will draw the view directly in front of them in as much detail as possible. Try to use the principles of aerial perspective to suggest the illusion of deep space.

2 In the art room assemble the drawings according to their appropriate position in the circle. What type of space do you experience when confronted with this group drawing?

Negative space drawing based on a real object

1 Cut out a small rectangle or square in the middle of a sheet of art paper. You will be using this as a viewfinder for this experiment.

2 Select an object in the room such as a plant, chair or projector. To make this exercise easier you may wish to position the object in front of the window. Focus the object in the middle of your viewfinder as you would with a camera. Allow the edges of the object to touch at least three sides of the frame. What happens if you extend your arm and the viewfinder towards the object? What happens as you draw it back towards you?

3 We are going to draw the negative spaces only. These are the spaces around the object. The areas where you can see light or gaps. Whilst looking at the object, carefully transfer the information with a pencil line on to a sheet of paper the same shape but larger in size than the viewfinder.

Experimenting with space using three-dimensional forms

1 Look closely at natural objects such as bones, shell, rocks, fruit or human forms. Do a series of sketches.

2 Explore the possibilities of opening up your sketches with negative spaces to create imaginative shapes. Translate this information into a sculpture, that is, create a three-dimensional form for your flat two-dimensional drawing.

3 Experiment with a variety of carving tools to carve the form from a solid block of wood, soapstone, sandstone, plaster etc. Observe the results. How does the negative space relate to the positive area?

4 Using natural objects or found objects (which may include discarded junk) create a three-dimensional sculpture using the assemblage technique. Design and assemble the sculpture in such a way that the sculpture moves through real space. The sculpture could be moved by air currents or by a motor.

5 Create a sculpture using any material and your choice of techniques which uses real space to separate the various components of the sculpture.

Perspective

Artists use perspective to create the **illusion of depth or space** on a flat surface.

Linear perspective is the most scientific method of creating the illusion of three-dimensional space. By using perspective we can establish the size of objects at different places in space. This mathematical system was developed during the 15th century.

The technique of perspective relies on some basic rules:

1 All lines in a composition, including those which are parallel, *appear* to meet at a common point in the distance when extended. (Although this does not happen in reality.)

2 This point is called the **vanishing point.**

3 The vanishing point is located on the **horizon line.**

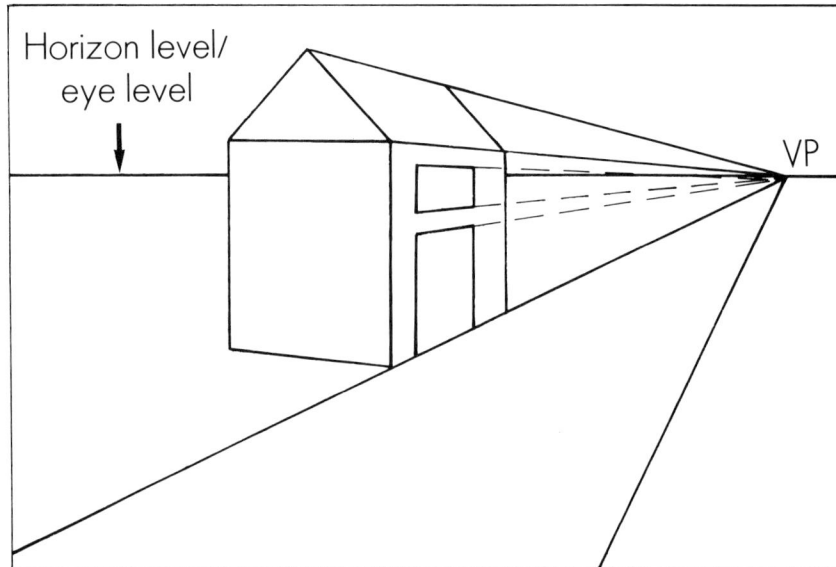

5 The vanishing point establishes the position of the viewer.

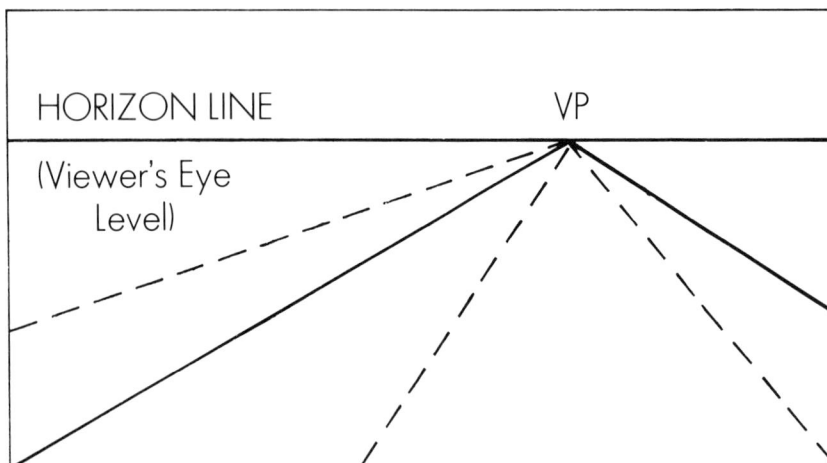

All parallel lines appear to meet at the same point.

4 The horizon line establishes the viewer's eye level.

MEINDERT HOBBEMA, *The Avenue, Middleharnis* 1689.
Oil on canvas. Reproduced by courtesy of the Trustees, The National Gallery, London.

Linear perspective is generally used for compositions containing architecture, whilst landscapes usually use aerial perspective. Look at the example above. This landscape was painted by the Dutch artist, Hobbema in 1689. It was one of the first paintings in which the beauty of the landscape is captured for its own value. The artist has used techniques of perspective to create an effect of spatial depth.

Questions

Are the following characteristics evident in this example:

1 Is there one vanishing point on the horizon line?

2 Do vertical lines become smaller in scale as they converge to the vanishing point?

3 Do parallel lines apper to meet at the vanishing point?

4 Is there more than one vanishing point?

81

Balance

Balance is one of the most important composition principles of design. Artworks are usually balanced visually using the elements of design such as line, shape, colour, texture, tone and direction, as weights. Repetition of shape, line and colour can be used to create balance.

There are two main types of balance:

Symmetrical balance

All shapes, lines, colours, etc are on one side of a central axis and are the mirror image of those on the other side. Repetition in a regular pattern creates symmetrical balance.

Asymmetrical balance

Shapes, lines and colours are balanced by using variety in size, tone or colour. For example, two small shapes may be used to equal one large shape. Repetition in an irregular pattern creates asymmetrical balance.

WESLEY JESSOP, student.

VAN TRUNG LUU, student.

Mady Daens

In this work *After the Quarrel* (1983) by Mady Daens the artist employs symmetrical balance. The two human forms are back to back along the central axis and are almost identical in pose and gesture. A repeat pattern along the bottom third of the painting is a unifying element that connects both halves of the painting as does the plain sky area.

The rounded form of the cloud (the only object in the sky) is a reflection of the rounded form of the cat. These forms balance each other as they are approximately the same distance in from the edge of the canvas.

Other elements which create balance in this work are the verticals of the human torsos in contrast with the horizontal sky line. The diagonals of the repeat pattern are reflections of the diagonals formed by the humans' legs.

MADY DAENS, *After the Quarrel* 1983.
Oil on paper, 28 x 38.5 cm. Collection of the artist.

Balance is also an important principle in the design of architecture.

Plan and photograph of New Parliament House, Canberra. Courtesy Parliament House Construction Authority.

The new Parliament House in Canberra is designed symmetrically on either side of a central axis. Entrance to the new Parliament House is through a forecourt, then through the symmetrically composed facade of the Great Verandah into a Reception Hall. The House of Representatives Chamber and offices on the left are balanced by the Senate Chamber and offices on the right. The central axis of the new Parliament House was designed to link directly with the existing provisional parliament building towards the south, and architecturally it reflects some of the stylistic characteristics of the older building. This creates a harmony and balance within the overall city plan for Canberra.

The new Parliament House, although designed along precise geometrical lines, sensitively harmonises with the site – it is built into the hill, rather than on it, so that it merges with the environment.

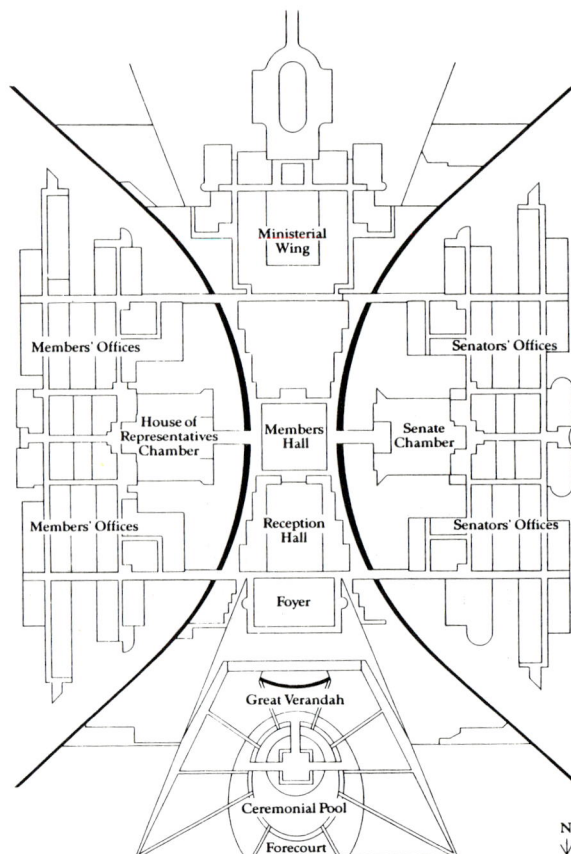

Ministerial Wing

Members' Offices

Senators' Offices

House of Representatives Chamber

Members Hall

Senate Chamber

Members' Offices

Reception Hall

Senators' Offices

Foyer

Great Verandah

Ceremonial Pool

Forecourt

N

Movement

KEITH HARING, Untitled 1982.
Synthetic polymer paint on vinyl tarpaulin, 213 x 220 cm. J W Power Collection.
Museum of Contemporary Art, Sydney.

Some works of art are said to be static or passive while others are active or create the effects of movement. Some art works actually do move, and these are referred to as **kinetic.**

Photographers can capture a moment in time – they can freeze the action of a football game or a dancer – capturing on film the type of movement involved with that activity.

Artists can also create the effect of action or movement. In figurative works of art, the pose taken by the figure can suggest a particular type of movement.

The bent arms and legs of the figure in the untitled work by Keith Haring create the effect of a walking or dancing type of movement. The repeated curved lines that spring out behind the feet, appear to act as sound waves or ripples that echo the movement. This figure appears to be a very active, noisy individual.

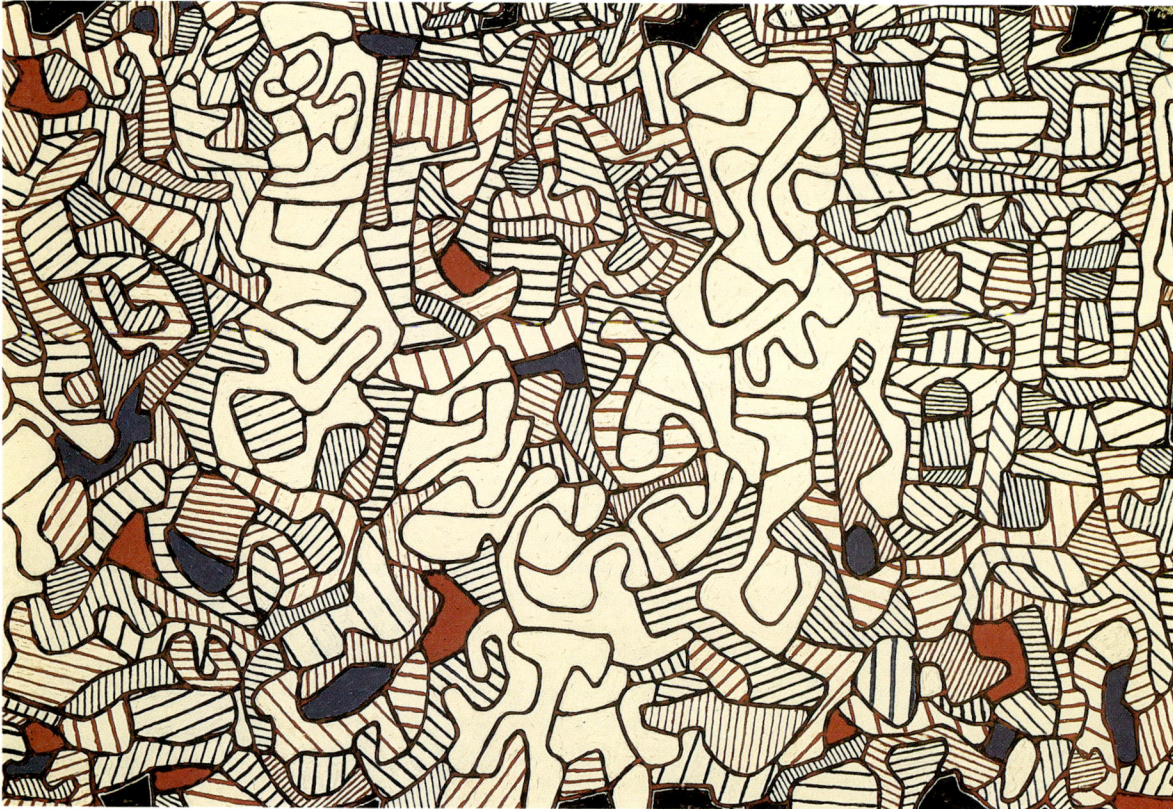

JEAN DUBUFFET, *Les Inconsistances* 1985 (detail, panel No. 4).
Synthetic polymer paint on four canvases installation 130 x 780 cm, each panel 130 x 195 cm.
Collection: Australian National Gallery, Canberra.
© ADAGP, Paris, 1988.

Lesley Dumbrell (born 1941)

Lesley Dumbrell manipulates forms and colours in an intellectual way. Her large scale works are concerned with changing qualities of light at different times of day and during different seasons. She is sensitive to the effects these changes have on the intensity of colours.

Although her paintings are abstract, they are suggestive of living forms. The artist's immediate environment has been a focus for her later paintings. The intensity of juxtaposed colours in her small garden adjacent to her studio has been a source of inspiration for her work. Her paintings are specifically about the colours she sees affected by the Melbourne light.

After working for two years in Italy, Lesley feels she is more sensitive to the unique quality of Australian light. The familiar is no longer taken for granted but understood with a fresh approach.

Jean Dubuffet (born 1901)

Jean Dubuffet's work is concerned with materials and surface quality. The subjects of his paintings are crude and naive forms, which seem to evolve naturally from the assemblage and construction of debris or mixed media on canvas.

Dubuffet's direct manipulation of material to create a strange and awkward image was influenced by the Surrealists and the artist's collection of the art of children and the mentally ill – 'Art Brut'. Dubuffet's work expresses his belief in the value of spontaneity and originality as seen in amateur work.

In both these non-figurative abstract works the effect of busy agitated movement is created through the repetition of straight or curved lines and of small shapes. The eye of the viewer is kept busy, jumping rapidly from form

LESLEY DUMBRELL, *Study for Taffetas 2* 1983.
Watercolour with some Chinese white, 65.9 x 103.4 cm. Collection of Simon Parr.

to form, looking for something to stop
on as a focal point – but none exists.
The eye is in constant movement –
moving restlessly over the canvas,
creating an almost dizzying and
nauseating effect on the viewer.

GASTON LACHAISE, *Floating Figure* 1927.
Bronze, 135 x 233 x 57 cm, cast 1979 by Modern Art Foundry, New York. No. 5 of an edition of seven.
Collection: Australian National Gallery, Canberra.

The sculpture *Floating Figure* can be found in the Sculpture Garden of the Australian National Gallery. The soft curvilinear contours of this figure flow in a basically horizontal direction. This type of line and direction creates a type of movement which is peaceful and relaxed, rather than dynamic or energetic. The form appears to be floating on the surface of the pond. Even though the figure is very solid and voluptuous, an effect of weightlessness is created by the elegant tapering of the limbs to small, delicate feet and hands.

Similar rhythmically undulating lines in *The Spirit of the Plains,* emphasise the graceful movement of the flight of the birds across the picture space.

SYDNEY LONG, *The Spirit of the Plains* 1914.
Oil on canvas, 76.8 x 153.7 cm. Collection: Australian National Gallery, Canberra.

WASSILY KANDINSKY, *Composition* 1922.
Colour lithograph, 28 x 24 cm. No. 8 from the portfolio of 12 Kleine Welten.
Collection: Australian National Gallery, Canberra.
©ADAGP, Paris and DACS, London 1988.

Wassily Kandinsky
(1866-1944)

A Russian-born painter who worked in Munich, Kandinsky was a pioneer of abstraction in painting. Kandinsky's early works reveal an intense interest in nature. Some of these works show the influence of the colour used by the Fauves. In his later works his aim was not to depict objective reality but rather a harmony of colour and form.

Kandinsky believed that the creative force in art should have its basis in the human spirit – that the artist could make a spiritual statement through line, colour, space and movement. He began to use musical titles such as 'Composition', 'Improvisation' and 'Lyrical' for his paintings, believing painting to be closely associated to musical expression. The style became known as abstract expressionism.

Dynamic energy and explosive movement are created in this painting through the use of strong diagonal lines and dramatic sweeping curves. The energy tends to focus itself at the points where the lines intersect, then explodes outwards towards the edges of the composition. In other parts of the painting, movement of a different kind is happening. In the top left-hand corner a few squiggly, snake-like lines appear to wriggle across the canvas.

Moving sculptures

In the motorised art works of Jean Tinguely (born 1925) the forms actually move like a machine. However, unlike machines, the movement of his forms have no function, nor do they move smoothly or rhythmically – they usually judder and jump in a rather hilarious, awkward manner.

JEAN TINGUELY, *Meta-Mecanique (Meta-Herbin)* 1954-1955.
Painted steel, electric motor, 174 x 108.7 x 81.7 cm. Collection: Australian National Gallery, Canberra.

Robert Woodward has created sculptures using moving water as the main sculptural element. The sculptures do not merely incorporate water, but rather they have the moving water as their essence.

Forecourt Cascades combines solid geometric blocks of stone, which create a planar pattern of tilted shapes, with the rhythmic flow of crystal clear water. Woodward has contrasted the solid mass of man-carved stone with the elusive qualities of the transparent moving water, creating an ever-changing pattern of sparkling light and reflections. The sculpture also incorporates the bubbling, gurgling sounds of cascading water.

ROBERT WOODWARD, *Forecourt Cascades* 1980.
South Australian grey speckled granite and water. High Court, Canberra.

Mobiles

Mobiles move in a complex rhythm with every current of air. The amount of motion may vary.

Alexander Calder, in the 1930s, was the first sculptor to create a new type of abstract sculpture which could float without being attached to a base or anchored to earth.

He called this a **mobile.** Mobiles are constantly changing as air currents cause the forms to twist and turn in space.

Mobiles may be constructed to allow individual components to rotate independently. Sound can also be incorporated, adding to the sensory experience of the viewer. (See section on mobiles for construction methods.)

Night and Day is suspended high from the ceiling of the National Gallery in Canberra. It moves with currents of air flowing through the gallery space. A strong spotlight highlights the brilliant colours of this carefully balanced abstract artwork, creating a projected shadow on the wall nearby.

As the mobile shifts in the air currents the shadow also changes form creating a separate two-dimensional constantly changing image. This section is an integral part of the sculpture: the artist's intention being that the shadow forms symbolise the subdued tones of night while the colourful forms of the sculpture itself symbolise the day.

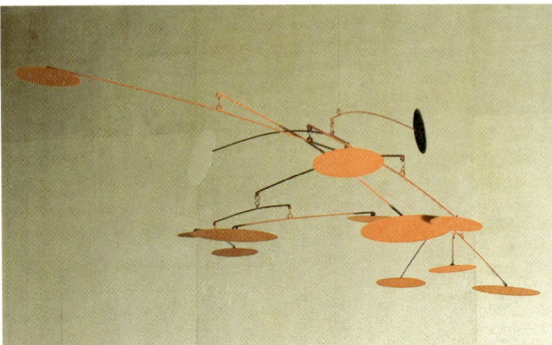

ALEXANDER CALDER, *Night and Day* 1964.
Painted steel, 73.5 x 333 x 330 cm.
Collection: Australian National Gallery, Canberra.

Movement Exercises

1 Choose three different types of music:
   - soft, flowing music
   - jumpy beat, disco or funky music
   - dynamic, dramatic, explosive music such as heavy metal.

Close your eyes and listen to each one separately. Play each one a few times to feel the mood each one creates. Draw up three squares in your sketchbook. Using the elements of line, shape and direction try to put these sounds into visual images.

Now create an abstract design which incorporates all three moods within the one design. What colours would you choose to recreate the mood of each type of music? Use these colours in your design. You could use paints, pastels, crayons or coloured pencils.

2 Collect pictures from newspapers or magazines of figures in action — sports, athletics, ballet, etc. Visit a physical education class or afternoon sport to watch the movements of students during games. Take action photos for later use.

Bring to class your favourite dance music and play it on a cassette player. Listen to the music and get a feel for the movements you use when dancing to the music. Get the whole class and the teacher involved; have an impromptu dance session. Take photos of the figures in movement, using a flash to freeze the action if there is not enough light.

From your collection of figures choose a number of figures to combine together to create an interesting composition. Do a quick contour sketch of the figures on a large sheet of art paper.

Using a harmony of angular or curvilinear lines work over the contour lines of the figures with a variety of thick and thin black lines, simplifying by emphasising main direction lines and eliminating other lines. Simplify face, hair and hands. Using black pen or texta, experiment with tonal gradation on the figures and complete with harmonious washes of colour, also using tonal gradation.

PART 2
THEMES FROM YOUR ENVIRONMENT

The School Environment

Abstract design

1 Walk around the school. In your sketchbooks make drawings of at least six different textures, patterns, lines and shapes, in either man-made or natural forms.

2 Develop a design by putting a 2 cm border around a large sheet of art paper and dividing your page into a number of areas. Your dividing lines may be straight or curved. Use variety in creating your areas; make some small or thin, others large or wide.

3 Fill in the areas with some of the textures and shapes from your sketchbook, repeating them to form a pattern. Some areas should be simple, others complex with lots of detail, to create contrast. Balance these two types of areas throughout the design. Use detailed areas to create focal points.

View from the school/view into the school

1 Sit inside the school playground and record your view as you look through the fence at the world outside the school, from the inside looking out. Include close details of the fence in your drawing.

2 Create a second drawing recording the view from the outside looking in. Emphasise a variety of linework, tone, texture and pattern.

3 Extend the information in your detailed drawing to create an etching printed in one colour.

Corridor viewpoint

The corridors of a school evoke a strange mood when the pupils are working inside the classrooms.

1   Locate an interesting viewpoint of a corridor in your school.

2   Do a quick sketch of the scene.

3   Complete a second drawing, this time in perspective. Try to create depth or distance in your drawing.

4   Draw the same corridor from another viewpoint, for example, looking down from the stairwell.

5   Select one of your drawings and choose lines, colours and a painting technique which suggests a still, quiet location.

Extension – still life arrangement of school satchels

1   Focus on one small section of the corridor. Create a series of sketches depicting a variety of school satchels in a random arrangement on the floor outside the classroom (include at least five or six bags). Look closely at the variety of shapes, textures and areas of light and shadow. What qualities do the bags possess? Are they stiff and rigid? Or are they soft and saggy? Are they crammed with books, bulging and overflowing or empty and limp? Are the bags neatly arranged in an orderly manner or thrown in a casual disarray? Are some of the bags overlapping or partially concealing others? In what direction are the bags leaning or slumped?

2   Experiment with composition. Draw three variations of your original drawing.
   (a) Include a small section of the wall behind the bags and include some of the floor. Include shadows, details of wall and floor patterns and textures.
   (b) Create a larger area of the wall and allow the bags to become smaller and more insignificant.
   (c) Zoom in and enlarge the bags so that they touch at least three sides of the frame of your paper. The bags should take up the entire composition.

3   Extend your sketches into a painting or coloured drawing using crayon pastels or coloured pencils or a combination of all these.

Try to emphasise the character of each bag. Remember each school satchel is as individual as its owner.

Another area of focus could be the school bike area or compound.

Three-dimensional extension of still life with a school object

Using your sketches and coloured drawings extend your information further to develop a work in three dimensions. Recreate as accurately as possible the same arrangement in a different material, for example, fabric such as hessian, canvas or calico which could be hand-painted or coloured. This may take the form of a soft sculpture, papier-mâché, clay, wire, mod-rock, moulded hand-made paper etc.

Found textures in the school environment

1   Collect a series of rubbings from different locations in your school environment, for example, signs, brick walls, lockers, desks, pathways, wire fences, the carpark, gates.

2   Cut up and reassemble to create a textured collage. A variation of this experiment could be the inclusion of sections of black and white photographs from the school environment with the textured patterns, to create a photomontage.

Pointillist painting of the art room

1   Using a viewfinder scan the art room for an interesting viewpoint. For example, you may focus on the area around the window sill and sink. Do not rearrange furniture or untidy elements as these may add interest to the composition. Include objects of varying sizes and interesting shapes, for example, stacked palettes, jars, paintbrushes, plants.

2   Record the information in the form of a large sketch.

3   We are now going to use the pointillist technique to extend your view of the art room into a painting. (Look at the technique in the works of Seurat and the Australian artist Grace Cossington-Smith).

4   You will need to mix a wide range of warm

and cool colours in light and dark tones.

5 Using a small brush or the end of your paint brush dab the dots of colour onto your painting to build up a mass of tiny areas of colour. Remember to apply warm colours for the areas advancing toward us and cooler colour combinations for areas of shadows. Avoid hard outlines. Experiment with the mixing of the colours and vary the size of the dots or your brush strokes.

Using an unusual viewpoint to record groups of students

1 Looking down from an upstairs classroom, record your observations of students standing, sitting or playing in the playground.
Draw the pupils exactly as you see them from above, in groups or isolation, standing or sitting.
(a) Sketch quickly.
(b) Record with photographs.

2 Extend into a painting or drawing, looking at qualities of shape, tonal contrasts, for example, shadows on pavement and space between and around the figures. Experiment with blurred effects to create an impression of movement. What effects can you achieve by adjusting the space between the figures?

3 Observe pupils in groups in the following places, from a variety of angles: queuing in the canteen, sitting on the grass eating lunch, playing handball, playing touch football, at assembly, walking home, working in the library.

Collage

1 Look at some works by Picasso and Braque, to provide inspiration.

2 Using any drawing you have made of the art room or other parts of the school, create a collage to recreate this image. Use cardboard, newspaper, magazine print materials, a variety of drawing and painting materials and rubbings of the floor and wall textures.

Transformation of an object

1 Students could work in small groups for this experience. Select an object or item of furniture from the art room, for example, chair, stool, table, overhead projector, window, door, etc. Using bags of recycled materials change the physical appearance and function of this object to give it a new sculptural identity.

2 Experiment with twisting, winding, wrapping and hanging materials such as wire, string, plastic, cellophane, canvas, strips of material, wool etc. For more permanent change to the object use mod-rock (material soaked in plaster) paint, papier-mâché, etc.

The Home Environment

Bedroom impression

Your bedroom is a reflection of you, your likes, collections, belongings. It suggests something of your personality. It is your private space.

The following experiments will require you to look at your bedroom much more closely than you have before.

1   If there is a mirror in your bedroom position yourself at an angle so as to allow yourself a view of the room. Sketch, in detail, all objects existing in the space that you can see in the mirror. Include the frame of the mirror.

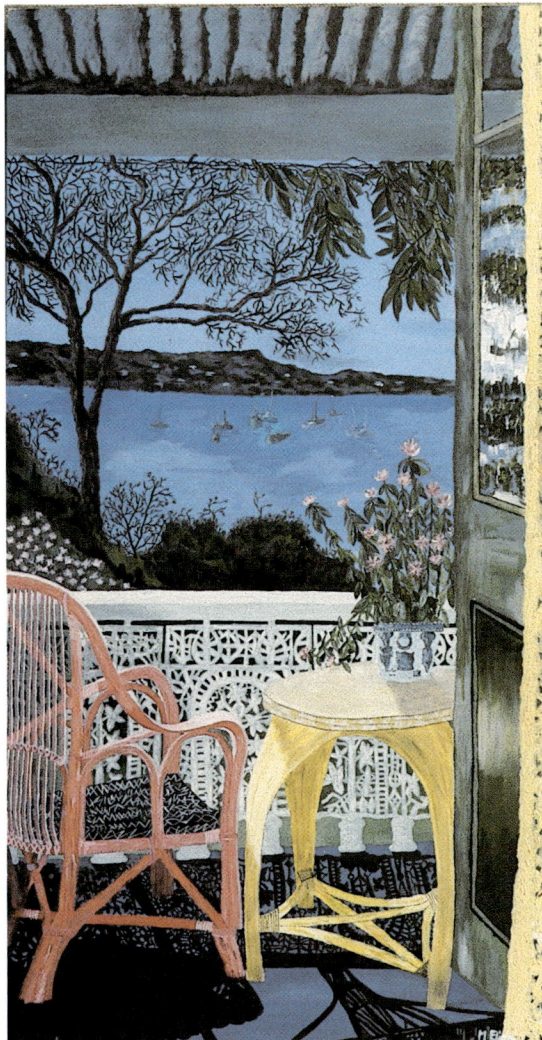

MONIKA ELISKA, student.

2   Do a second drawing with yourself depicted in the centre of the mirror with your bedroom surrounding you.

3   Extend one of your drawings into a painting,

exploring different techniques of applying the paint, for example, pointillism, soft watercolour, etc. This exercise could also be explored through photography.

Looking out through your bedroom window

1   Look at the view from your bedroom window. Do a detailed drawing of the view you can see. Include all objects no matter how mundane, for example cars parked across the street, clothesline, trees planted against the wall or a paling fence.

2   Use linework and a fine-point felt pen to extend information on patterns and textures you observe. Create a feeling of distance and perspective, by creating very clear detail to describe areas which are close to your viewpoint and less clear detail as the distance increases.

3   Try experimenting with your composition (arrangement of the information you wish to present). Decide on a focal point. Which direction do you wish to lead the viewer's eye? You may decide to include the frame of the window and part of the interior of the room in your drawing.

4   Use your first drawing as the basis for a painting in which you will use two different painting techniques. One technique for the interior and one technique for the outside view.

Photo-montage of an interior

1   Using a camera and black and white film, take numerous photographs of your bedroom from different angles and viewpoints.

2   Organise these photographs into an interesting arrangement, perhaps overlapping or cutting into photographs.

3   Select one image in each photograph which will become the focal point. Carefully colour this image with watercolours so that it creates a contrast with the surrounding black and white area.

Relief print

1   Do a drawing of part of a room in the home.

Concentrate on line, shape, and space – try to see everything in black or white. Use a hole, cut in a piece of cardboard as a viewfinder, to limit your area of focus.

2   Transform this drawing into a negative space drawing, that is, reverse your tones so that light becomes dark and dark becomes light.

3   Develop this drawing into an interesting design suitable for a relief print in which shape and line dominate. Experiment with different textures, for example, wool, hessian, string, corrugated cardboard. Glue down your shapes, then print and evaluate the result.

TANYA WHEELER, student.

The Natural Environment

Direct observation

1   As a class group discuss your local environment. What proportion of your local area remains natural? What criteria would you use when classifying an area as the natural environment? Is there any natural bush left? Are there only man-made parks? Why do we have them?

2   List characteristics of living things which exist as part of the natural environment and record your observations and sensory experiences.

3   Explore your local environment. Take cameras and sketchbooks. Look for interesting photos — close-ups of plants, flowers, the bark of a tree, etc. Do some rubbings of natural textures. Collect samples of natural materials, for example, dry leaves, twigs, sand, dirt, etc. Make maps of the area, tape record bush noises, research the history of the area. Return to the same location at different times of day. Note the changes in colour, light and composition.

Collage

Using your natural materials, rubbings, photos and drawing materials, create an interesting abstract collage. Consider the elements and principles of design when you consider the composition of the collage.

Design

Use a hole cut in a piece of paper as a viewfinder, and placing it over bark or a piece of ground, draw an enlargement of what you see. Develop this drawing into a small design painted in earthy tones.

Printmaking

1   Using natural specimens found on location, examine them closely under a magnifying glass.

2   Do a series of diagrammatic drawings. Extend these drawings to create
    (a)   a very realistic image
    (b)   a semi-abstract image based on the same specimen (a wildflower or native plant).

3   Use your abstract design as a motif for any of the following techniques of printmaking: lino printing, woodblock printing, silk-screen printing or batik. Look at the work of the Australian artist Margaret Preston for inspiration.

JOHN FABIEN, student.

Batik

This unit of work is based on the concept of growth in nature.

1   Go out into the park, garden, or courtyards in your school where plants are growing.

2   Draw and photograph living forms — life lines on trees, surface pattern of bark, flowers sprouting from stems, buds and seed pods on trees.

99

3 Evaluate your drawings and photos. Create a composition in which life and growth seem to burst forth exuberantly from a multitude of living things. Simplify your forms so that the design is suitable for a batik wall hanging. Cotton lawn or silk are suitable materials for batik. Use a mixture of 50 per cent beeswax and 50 per cent paraffin wax, or obtain specially blended waxes from batik suppliers. Djantings (instruments for applying wax) or fine brushes can be used to apply hot melted wax to outlines around forms. Many other methods of applying wax can be used to create patterns and textures on the batik, for example, sponges, wide brushes, toothbrushes, the edge of thick cardboard, etc.

Fibre reactive dyes (eg Drimarene dyes) that are painted on by hand with a brush produce the best results for a wide range of pure colours, from intense bright hues to pastels. Completed works must be dried (using Drimarene dyes) before a fixing substance (Drimafix) is painted on the surface. The work must then be rolled up in plastic and left to set for 24 hours, rinsed then dried again.

Changing environment

1 Focus on a particular area of the natural environment and take your paints, coloured pencils or pastels to the location.

2 Capture your impressions of that area at different times of day, in different light conditions, on three separate canvas boards or on cardboard. Work within a time limitation, perhaps 30 minutes for each painting. Keep your observations quick and spontaneous. Look at the paintings by Turner, Constable and Monet.

Miniature environment

Explore an area inhabited by tiny creatures or plant forms, for example, a rock pool, freshwater pond, cave or garden bed.
Do detailed studies of these creatures. You may wish to simplify their forms.
Create a painting or coloured drawing capturing them in their own environment. Experiment with colours, perhaps electric colours or softer pastels. Emphasise unusual shapes, line work and patterns. This work could be in the form of an abstract or semi-abstract composition.

Living creatures and their environment

1 Explore differences between living creatures and their environment. For example reflections on the surface of water and swimming fish or insects camouflaged against rocks or trees.

2 Look at a living creature which is well camouflaged against its environment. Create a series of abstract colour designs which explore different surface patterns and colours.

3 These could be extended as major works on canvas or fabric, using techniques such as batik or fabric printing.

Patterns from nature

1 Look closely at different areas of nature such as — bark on trees, sunlight filtering through treetops, a waterfall, sand-dunes and rocks, patterns and reflections on the surface of water.

2 Reproduce as accurately as possible the patterns, textures, tones and colours you can see with a variety of media — pastel, wax crayon, water colour, pencils, inks etc. When each area is complete cut out sections of each effect in a variety of shapes and sizes.

3 Arrange into an exciting collage which highlights similarities and differences in the patterns.

Natural sculpture

1 Choose at least six natural forms, for example, leaves, shells, pebbles, seedpods, twigs, pine cones etc.

2 Collect a variety of specimens in each category, for example, different sized and coloured leaves, differently textured seed pods, different shaped twigs.

3 Create a sculpture using these collections. Consider how these forms could be combined and displayed.

Abstract sculpture

There are many ways of making sculpture. You are going to use a method which has been used since prehistoric times — carving — that is, a method of cutting away. The material you will use is soapstone, a very easy material to carve. You are going to create a sculpture based on the abstract forms you can see in your piece of soapstone. Try to create organic forms.

1 Study your piece of soapstone. Look at the main shape — is it rounded, oval, irregular? Does the surface of the stone have any raised areas, lines or shapes?

2 Now you are going to start carving your soapstone. Your teacher can explain how to use the various carving tools. As you carve, emphasise the main shape or forms you can see in your block; for example, if it is oval, then carve away any small irregular pieces and create a smooth curved form. Is the surface flat or are there undulating forms you could emphasise, are there forms you can carve in relief?

3 As you work look at your sculpture, and evaluate it. Is it taking on a living, organic form? Is it interesting from all angles? Is the surface pleasing to touch? Make some parts rough and some parts smooth if it suits your form. Would lines carved into your form suit it? To finish the surface, refer to the section on soapstone carving.

Ceramics

In this unit of work you are going to create two related ceramic forms using the theme of the environment. Your ceramic forms may be:

(a) functional pottery, eg containers, vases, bottles, teapots etc, decorated with themes from the environment.

(b) sculptural forms — based on the environment.

You could use any number of techniques to create your forms — slab, mould, coil. The two forms must be related by either the technique or by the decoration. The theme for this work is the environment:

(a) man-made environment — industrial forms, buildings, mechanical shapes, sharp, straight, clean forms.

(b) natural environment — trees, plants, flowers, organic, flowing, curved forms — textures resembling earth and bark, etc.

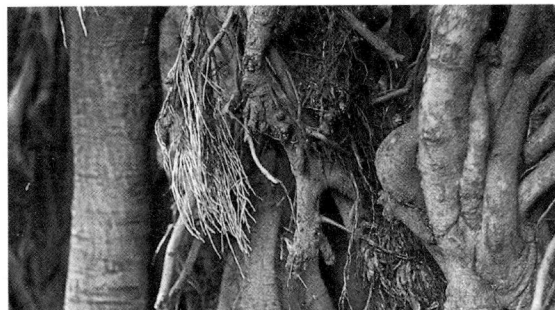

1 Make a decision about what aspect of the environment you are basing your work on.

2 Make drawings/designs in your sketchbook of your major work ideas — make brief notes on the techniques and possible decoration you will use. Remember the importance of thorough joining techniques, particularly in slab building forms.

3 As work progresses evaluate the surface treatment. Do you decorate before the clay is dry? If you are using impressing, incising, slip, or appliqué as decoration you will need to do this before it dries. Oxides and glazes are applied to a bisque fired form. Finished works are dried, fired, glazed and refired.

The Man-made Environment

The built environment

1 Make a series of drawings and photographs of several different styles of windows, doorways, verandahs and fences you can find in the built environment. Focus on how they relate to the structure in terms of line, tone, texture, etc. Focus also on details or parts of the subject matter, eg doorhandles and knockers, window casements, shutters and internal coverings, gateways in fences, stairs leading up to porches and verandahs, awnings over windows and verandahs, letterboxes in fences, etc.

2 Evaluate your drawings and photos. Select your most interesting images. Organise these into a series which could be suitable subject matter for a series of designs, prints or larger drawings. The series could focus on the various elements of a particular style in the built environment (eg federation style, or revival styles in civic structures); or the series could focus on the variety of styles found in one particular element (eg gateways and fences); or the series could relate images through certain dominant elements such as line, tone, direction and texture.

3 Evaluate your drawings and photos again. Does one image come across strongly in terms of interesting composition, tonal contrast, texture, etc? Consider this image on a large scale, filling a canvas. Would certain details or elements need to be reorganised, eliminated or added to make the painting more interesting? Experiment with colour schemes, tonal qualities and paint application techniques before starting the painting.

Mechanical objects

1 Draw or photograph close-up sections of a car or bike from a variety of viewpoints. Try to contrast areas of detail with unpatterned areas. Organise images into a composition suitable for a silk-screen print in a minimum of three colours or tones.

2 This approach could be developed into a series of silk-screen prints for a major art work by extending the theme to include other mechanical or man-made objects found in our environment, such as lawnmowers, mechanical pool cleaners, children's toys such as three-wheeler bikes and trucks, vacuum cleaners, cassette players, food mixers, toasters, typewriters, computers, etc. Photographic silkscreen techniques could supplement paper-cut stencil and lakron or autotype lacquer film stencil techniques.

The city

1 Visit the city with your camera and sketchbook. Photograph and draw various aspects typical of the hustle and bustle of the city streets – busy intersections, neon signs, advertising billboards, pedestrian plazas, newsstands, bus-stops, street lights, signs, vehicles and pedestrians. Look for interesting combinations of lines, tones, patterns, shapes, etc. Restrict your viewpoint by making close-up observations of forms.

RIM LEE, student.

2 Evaluate your photographs and drawings. Combine several aspects or viewpoints of the city in a design suitable for a large wall-hanging that uses batik, silkscreen printing, appliqué or other fabric design techniques.

Communication

1 Take an excursion into the city and one around the suburbs. List, sketch and photograph as many different aspects of communication you can find in the environment.
Some examples are:

- telephone and power poles
- broadcasting communication towers
- satellite discs
- street signs, pedestrian signs, parking signs
- traffic control lights and signs
- destination and time boards at railway stations
- loudspeakers
- arrivals and departures boards at airports
- airtraffic control towers

2 List, sketch and photograph subject matter which relates directly to the communication of information and actions taken in relation to the information communicated. Some examples are:
- the image of pedestrians' feet crossing in accordance with walk signs
- car brake lights or turning indicators in accordance with traffic signals or signs
- a mouth talking into a telephone

3 Organise your images into categories. For example:
- telecommunication — telephone, television, radio
- traffic and pedestrian control
- transport — train, air, bus, ferry

Create a series of designs on the theme of **communication** showing its various aspects in our modern technological world.

Industry

1 Take an excursion to explore your local industrial area. Draw and photograph various elements in the industrial landscape. For example:
- factory buildings and yards
- warehouses
- piles of materials and products such as wood, scrap metal, pipes, etc
- building sites and cranes

2 Evaluate your images. Your explorations could form the basis of further investigations for a photographic series. Focus attention in particular on tonal, textural and linear qualities. Remember that correct light exposure and interesting composition through the viewfinder are the basis of good photography.

3 Process film and make a series of contact prints. Which are the most successful? Which ones need to be cropped? Print some of your best photos. Experiment with some creative darkroom techniques such as tone drop-outs, sepia toning and photo-montage (combining several images within one photo).

4 Evaluate your experiments and organise your

photos into a series in which the photos are related by a particular element or technique. Try not to be repetitive with your imagery.

5 Your explorations could form the basis of a series of wood cut or lino cut prints. Textural and linear qualities could be emphasised.

Workplaces

1 Take an excursion to the local commercial and business district and shopping area. Photograph people in their work environment. Make some quick sketches of the environment of each work place. Some examples are:
- smash repair shops
- garages
- shops (eg green grocers, delicatessen, supermarket, butcher, liquor stores, newsagents)
- weekend markets
- car sales yards

2 Develop and print photos. Evaluate prints and sketches. This theme could be the starting point for a painting, a mixed media work, relief sculpture, a series of drawings, a series of photos, or a series of silk-screen prints.

Advertising

1 Consider the role advertising plays in our society. What types of markets do advertisers appeal to? Youth/beauty/sex/wealth/happiness/security/action/yummy? How does the advertising change to appeal to the different market groups? Look at some different advertisements in magazines and newspapers and on television. Who is the advertisement aimed at and how does it convince the audience?

2 You are going to design an image and advertising campaign for an imaginary pop group. With your friends take photos of yourselves. Make a few photocopies for use in several aspects of the campaign, for example: album cover, poster and magazine story.

3 Make up a name for your pop group. Consider what sort of music you play and what image you want to project to the public, for example, punk, heavy metal, funk, blues, etc. Using your photo collection, draw your group dressed in stage clothes. Design an album cover for your group. Analyse album cover layouts. Which ones are most successful? Consider lettering and other design elements such as balance, contrast, spatial qualities and colour. Make up some song titles for your album. Design a poster for a concert or gig at which you are going to perform. Information that should be included along with your band's name is date, time and venue. Get together with your friends and write a magazine article by interviewing members of the band. Include photos of band members, a title for the story and the interviewer's name.

The Human Form

Observation drawings

1 Using pencil or fine-point texta, create a series of drawings of the different components of your body without looking at the paper as you draw. Follow the contours of these parts with your eyes as your other hand draws a corresponding line onto a sheet of paper. Discuss the results. How do the results differ to your usual drawings?

2 Use the same technique mentioned above to create a blind contour drawing of your face. Feel the contours of your face as you draw.

3 Using a large sheet of paper complete a life size drawing of yourself feeling the component parts as you go or by looking in the mirror as you draw.

Modified contour drawing

1 Look at the hand you don't draw with. Watch how its position and gesture changes if you do the following actions with it:
(a) holding a ruler
(b) picking up a pin
(c) slap the desktop
(d) clench your fist
(e) hold an imaginary flower
(f) put your hand around a round ball (eg cricket ball)
(g) hold a piece of paper
(h) walk two fingers across the desk

2 Now make a drawing of four of these positions. Look carefully at your hand. Can you see all of the fingers or are some parts hidden? How long is each finger? Is one finger bigger than another?
Make sure you don't change your viewpoint (position of your head) during each drawing.

Homework

Do two modified drawings of your own foot, with or without a shoe, in two different positions.

Component parts

Look at one particular component of the human body in close detail. For example the thumb, the big toe, the ear, the nose, the eye.
(a) Divide your sheet of paper into a regular or irregular grid and experiment with different mediums.
(b) Record your observations of this subject in charcoal, pastel, photograph, graphite pencil, wax resist and ink.
(c) Try looking at the same subject from different viewpoints.
(d) Divide a large sheet of paper into a grid — regular or irregular and arrange these works into an interesting organisation of images which illustrate contrasts and similarities of form, shape, colours and textures.

Negative space drawing (perceiving the shape of spaces)

1 Cut the shapes of a human figure or group of figures from a magazine or newspaper. Stick onto a small sheet of paper so that part of the figure(s) touch at least two edges of the paper.
Note: the shape or format of the paper should be suitable for the overall shape of the figure(s).
Now observe all the spaces around the figures. Outline all these spaces to emphasise that they are shapes of spaces.

2 On a larger sheet of paper, in the same format as the smaller one, draw the negative spaces that you have carefully observed and outlined on the smaller sheet, enlarging them to fit into the larger sheet.

3 The positive forms and the negative spaces share the same edges. Shade or fill in these negative spaces. See how the negative space defines the positive space shapes. Now complete the details inside the forms.

Funny sayings/similes

1 Consider sayings such as:
• I've got my eye on you
• What an eyeful
• That one is on the nose
• What an earbashing
• What a mouthful
• He's as skinny as a rake
• She waddles like a duck
• Fingernails like claws

- What a tongue-lashing
- What a hair-raising experience

2 Can you think of any more that relate to the human form? Can you think of a way to make a visual image to go with these sayings?

Squashed face image/fantastic creature

This is an exercise using photographic paper and chemicals, and petroleum jelly (vaseline).

1 Prepare photographic chemicals beforehand in darkroom.

2 Smear petroleum jelly all over your face.

3 In the darkroom, in red or orange safety light only, take an imprint of your face by placing a piece of photographic paper over your face and press hard to lift an imprint of eyes, nose mouth and skin texture. Be careful not to slip as this will smudge the results.

4 Expose the photographic paper to white light for three seconds.

5 Develop, wash in warm water to remove petroleum jelly, then fix and wash again.

6 Evaluate your squashed face image, then use this print as the basis for an ink drawing of an imaginary fantastic creature.

Expressions

1 Look for examples of artists who, in their work, represent particular emotions through facial expression, body gestures and colour, eg:
- Picasso — *The Blindman's Meal, Guernica, Weeping Woman*
- Munch — *The Scream, Anxiety*
- Leonardo — *Mona Lisa*
- Frans Hals — *Malle Babbe*
- Rembrandt — *Self Portrait Laughing.*

2 Find art work that expresses the following: terror, happiness, sadness, distress, surprise, anger, loneliness, insanity.

3 Collect from newspapers, magazines and comic strips as many different facial expressions as you can find. Discuss with your classmates how the shapes and lines of the face and the directions of the mouth, eyes and eyebrows changes for each expression. Act out a number of different emotions using four facial expressions and body gestures to create mood.

4 Take photos of each other in a variety of expressions as individuals and in groups.

Develop and print your photos.

5 Draw several balloons in a line or in a bunch. Draw a face on each balloon so that each face shows a different emotional expression.

6 Choose an interesting face/expression from your total collection of photos and cut-outs. Choose from a variety of media — pitt pencils, coloured pencils, charcoal, cray-pas or textas, then draw the face you have chosen, emphasising the facial features through use of tonal contrast and texture. Create an appropriate abstract pattern and colour scheme in the background to further emphasise the emotion being depicted.
- This theme could be easily extended into a lino or woodblock print.

ADAM CLARK, student.

Self-portrait

1 Using a mirror study the characteristics of your face. What are your best and worst or most interesting features? Which aspects of your face do you feel illustrate your personality best? Which aspects would you emphasise if painting a self portrait?

2 Experiment with distortion.

3 Do a series of detailed studies of different expressions in the mirror.
(a) In the first series use only curving, twisting,

106

flowing lines. Look at the portraits by Van Gogh, Modigliani, El Greco, Leonardo da Vinci and Munch.

(b) In the second series use mainly straight, angular lines. Look at examples of portraits by the German Expressionists – Kirchner, Nolde and the Analytical Cubists.

Caricature drawing

1 Caricatures are found every day in the newspapers of politicians and other famous people. Collect some examples.

2 Using a mirror to look at your own face or choosing a classmate, analyse which characteristics are most prominent (eyes too small, nose too big) or those characteristics which make up the individuality of your personality or that identify your face as yours.

3 Using fine-point texta or biro draw the face as a caricature – ie exaggerate the facial features that are obvious or that identify the face. Use the cross-hatching method (see page 37) to create tonal gradation (ie areas of light and dark).

Photo-montage – distorted face

1 Make a 10 x 8 inch print from facial expression photos taken for expressions theme. Cut photo into 1 cm strips, number them so you don't lose any or mix them up. Rule up a large sheet of art paper with 1 cm wide strips. You should have twice as many strips as the photo.

2 Stick down your photo strips on every alternate strip on the art paper so that you have left gaps.

3 Using a soft lead pencil try to create the exact tones and patterns of the face by filling in the gaps, thus joining the parts of the face together. The result will be a stretched, distorted face.

4 Collect a variety of photocopied images of people. These may include photocopies of portraits painted by well known artists or simply photocopies of ordinary people. Cut these up into irregular sizes and shapes. Select at least four different shapes. Manipulate these shapes to create a new 'fantasy person'. The pieces will not form a complete person or face. Experiment with pencil or texta to draw back over parts of the photocopies and fill in the gaps. Try extending – facial features, overlapping cut pieces, adding textures and patterns of jewellery and clothing.

Photo-montage – create a mood environment

1 Take photos of each other acting out expressions. This time take the whole figure making sure body gestures also reflect your mood or expression. Develop and print photos into 10 x 8 inch size.

2 Cut out the figure(s) using a stencil knife and stick onto a sheet of art paper.

3 Try to visualise/imagine an environment that reflects the mood/gestures you are expressing (eg tearing your hair out in a maths lesson or laid back and relaxed on the beach). Draw in and colour this environment using materials of your choice.

Imagine yourself at 25? 45? 75?

Using three photocopies of photographs of your face, work over each image trying to imagine how you would look at 25, 45 and 75. Use any materials of your choice.

Changing your image

1 Take a black and white photograph of
   (a) your face or
   (b) your entire body.
   This exercise could be done by working in pairs in class. Print the results preferably as large as possible.

2 Using your finished black and white photograph reproduce at least four photocopies. Each of these images is going to be used to change your persona. Using your imagination and a variety of media, such as paint, collage, crayon, coloured pencil create your version of yourself on the photocopy as the following: Me as a **pop star,** Me as a **politician,** Me as an **athlete,** Me as a **socialite,** Me as a **punk,** Me as a **movie star.**

Fantasy self-portrait

Create a series of drawings of your own face, using a mirror, from various aspects. Combine these images by dissecting and overlapping your drawings. In the background areas which result include images from your dreams, your childhood or objects which are particularly important to you. Arrange all the images in an interesting way so as to unify the human image and the background images.

For inspiration look at the portraits of Chagall and Picasso. Avoid traditional rules of perspective, gravity, time, solidity. Experiment with a variety of techniques such as wax crayon, pen and ink, texta, collage, coloured pencil, water colour, pastels etc.

Life drawing from different viewpoints

Using a classmate as a model find an interesting viewpoint with your canvas stretcher positioned on an easel in front of you. If you are unable to use canvas try a large sheet of cardboard.

Using brush and paint or palette knife and paint, quickly draw your first impression of the figure.

Next, swap positions with one of your classmates and record your response to the figure from a new viewpoint overlapping the information. Record up to five or six viewpoints.

Your result will become an abstract network of complex lines.

Have you created any feeling or impression of movement?

Select colours which may or may not relate to the real colour scheme and paint into the new shapes made by the linework.

The application of colour may also be quick and spontaneous using one or more media, such as texta, crayon, pastel, paint, dye or impasto medium.

Images of people in society

1 Make a list of different groups of people you have seen in your local environment and through the media. What aspect of their appearance makes them recognisable as a particular group?
Groups of people who dress in a characteristic manner could include: punks, bikies, surfies, university students, politicians, teachers, teenagers, sportspeople, tourists, housewives and television stars.

2 Collect as many photographs and drawings of these groups as possible. Newspapers and special magazines would be useful.
Select a particular group and do simple observational sketches; preferably life drawings.
Particular attention should be given to characteristics such as facial expressions, clothing, hairstyles, stature, stance and age.

Major work extension

Using the information you have researched, interpret the characteristics of the group you chose as a mixed media study.

You may decide to create a caricature of the person or group.

Experiment with the scale of the work. A group of students may decide to create a life size mural.

Mixed media may include photography, collage using newspaper cut-outs, found objects, canvas, coloured paper etc.

Looking at the human form as it relates to its environment

1 Look at people as they interrelate with the natural and man-made environment. List examples in a brainstorming session in class, such as people lying on the beach sunbaking, people shopping in the supermarket, people sitting in cars in traffic at peak hour, queuing in the supermarket, pedestrians crossing the street.

2 Record your observations of these activities involving groups of figures by sketching or photography.

3 Make a collection of drawings and photographs based on the individual figure working or playing in their environment. For example, your mother preparing the dinner, washing up, relaxing in front of the television; your father shaving, washing the car, reading the paper.

4 Compare the sketches of groups with those of the individuals. What differences do the two have in terms of the placement of the figures and the use of space? Extend one or both subjects into more detailed studies.
Experiment with the way in which the figures relate to their surroundings and each other. Make decisions about the amount of space required for the background. Will the figure take up a large area of the total space?
Will the figure appear close-up or far away and insignificant?

Relief sculpture

Using any of your previous drawings of the human form design a composition for a high relief sculpture. Concentrate on a close-up format (eg head and shoulders). The forms will be built up using rolled or crumpled newspaper taped in position on a piece of masonite and papier-mâché over the top. The work can then be finished with paint or rubbed with shoe polish and varnished.

FREYA POVEY, *Sioux You.*
Courtesy of Crafts Council of Australia, The Rocks, Sydney.

Relief sculpture – clay

1   Draw a portrait of yourself or a friend. Refer to a photograph or draw direct from life, choosing either a realistic or caricature approach, depending on how you wish to portray yourself or friend in a relief sculpture.

2   Roll out a slab of clay and shape it to the outline shape of the face – round or oval depending on the type of face you are depicting.
    Drape this slab over a curved mould. A mould can be made with crumpled newspaper taped together and covered with plastic.
    Add pieces of clay and model these to form facial shapes. Use the sketch as your guideline.

3   Allow to dry, then fire. Glaze and then fire again.

Sculpture

Using found objects from your home, or factory cast-offs, assemble components to create a human form.

FREYA POVEY, *African Queen.*
Courtesy of Crafts Council of Australia, The Rocks, Sydney.

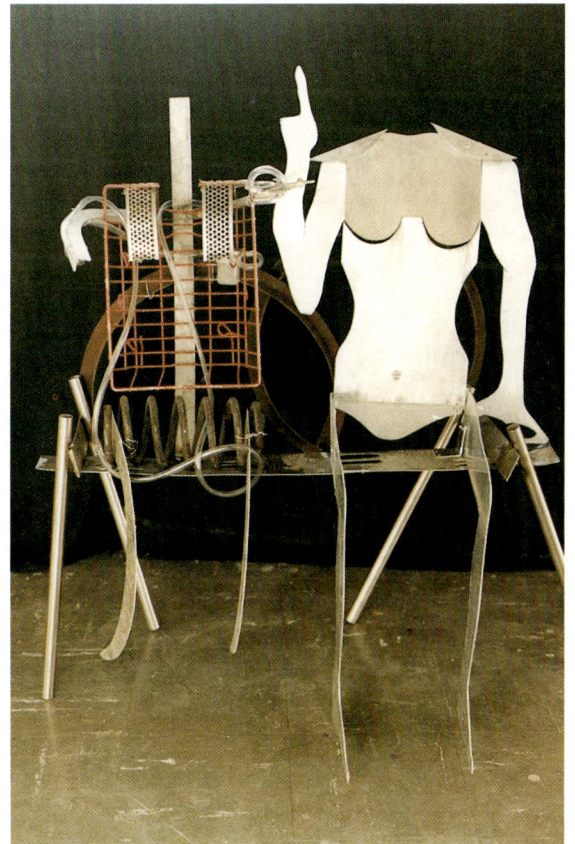

MATTHEW IRELAND, student.

109

Animals

A visit to the zoo

1 Walk around the zoo. Look closely at the different animals, the zoo environment and the enclosures.

2 Choose two animals, birds or reptiles that you really like. In your sketchbooks write down the name of each animal. What sort of environment does it normally live in? Jungle? Bushland? Underwater? What sort of environment has been created in the enclosure in which the animal is kept? What does the animal look like? What shape is it? What type of hair, or fur or pattern or skin? What sort of colours? How does the animal move? What sort of noises/sounds does it make to communicate? Make a drawing of the whole animal. Try drawing the general shape first. Add details last.

3 Make a close-up drawing of the animal's head showing more detail than the first drawing.

4 Draw a close-up of some of the vegetation you see in the enclosure with the animal.

Lino cut

1 Evaluate your zoo drawings. Create a design suitable for a lino cut. Simplify details and emphasise line and pattern. Try to include some of the natural vegetation. The lino cut design could be printed in up to five colours.

2 Transfer design to lino — fill most of the space available with your shapes. Carve away the outline of the shapes first, then print your first colour. Make at least five copies. Carve away more lino each time you wish to print another colour over the top of the originals. Make sure you register each new colour carefully over previous colours. When your series of five prints is finished choose the best print to mount and display.

Animal forms in clay

1 You are going to make clay animal forms using the pinch pot technique as the basic building technique. After you have prepared the clay divide into two equal parts. Roll clay into two balls. Using your thumb, press into the clay and open up a hole in the top. Start pinching your thumb and fingers together. At the same time rotate the clay ball with your other hand. Make sure the walls and the base of the pot

are of an even thickness. Both pots should be exactly the same shape.

2 The two pots are going to be joined to form a sphere. Roughen the surfaces to be joined with a sharp implement. Support both pots in one hand. Using the thumb of your other hand, drag some clay down over the join all around the circumference. Now smooth over the surface. Make sure that all your joins are solid and secure.

3 Features and limbs can be added to this basic form. Use your imagination for this work — you could create an imaginary animal that combines the features of several animals.
Once the form of the animal is complete, use modelling tools to texture the surface or add clay bits to create the impression of hair or fur or scales, etc.

4 Once the animal is complete you must cut a small hole somewhere so that the air trapped inside can escape during the firing process. The bisque fired form can be glazed and fired again.

Poster

1 Look at different types of visual communication — road signs, people signs (men's and women's toilets), company emblems. Look at some ways of depicting words through symbols, for example, arrows mean 'this way', skull and cross bones mean 'danger', a burning cigarette encircled with a cross through it means 'no smoking'.

2 Design and paint a poster which could be placed in a zoo to show people where a particular animal could be found. It is important to remember that you are not drawing the animal realistically but rather using a symbol that represents the animal. You cannot use any words in your poster.

Line drawings

1 Choose a living animal subject, preferably your pet. Perhaps a cat, dog, goldfish or bird. Do a series of quick observational sketches depicting the different positions of the animal over a period of time. Try to add to the drawings until you have depicted a series of sequential movements.

2 How would you describe the manner in which your particular animal moves? Is it flowingly graceful, very relaxed, agitated and stiff, or perhaps highly strung and nervous in its movements?

3 Extend one or more of your drawings into a large drawing using linework in keeping with the character of the animal chosen.

Extending a detailed line drawing into an etching

1 Using the information observed and recorded in the previous exercise, reduce to a small detailed drawing which emphasises fine linework. Experiment with different types of lines to create tonal values using cross-hatching. Emphasise patterns and textures with linework.

2 Transfer linear information onto a paper, plastic or aluminium etching plate using etching tools to inscribe the lines. Ink up and print.

Recording animals with a variety of media

1 Find a location where you can sketch your observations of animals directly. For example the zoo, local stable, paddock, farm, aviary or aquarium. Create a series of drawings using the following mediums:
- pen and ink washes
- conte crayon
- wax crayon
- watercoloured pencils/crayons
- pastels
- any combination of the above

2 Try to record the textures found in feathers, fur, skin; the colours of markings, distinguishing features, tonal patterns and any interesting body structures. Note the way in which the animal fits into its environment. In your work, record effects of movement if relevant.

Drawing animal subjects directly onto fabric

1 Go to your local or school library or wildlife park and research native Australian animals. Do a detailed study of one you have selected through a series of drawings. These could be drawings of the entire animal or close-ups of the animal's face. Look at their environment, as you may wish to include aspects of this in your drawing.

MATTHEW HOWLEY, student.

2 Using fabric crayons, refer to your research drawings as you transfer your information straight onto a T-shirt or other chosen fabric. Experiment with building up linework, mixing and overlapping colours and patterns to create a description of your animal. Try experimenting with fabric paint, brushes and sponges in addition to the crayons. Apply heat with your iron to make permanent and colour fast.

Planning a major work painting

1 Using your pet as a subject, again do a detailed study drawing of it, perhaps taking a photograph first as animals are not always co-operative subjects. Experiment with the composition of the drawing. Try to use most of the space available for the animal.

2 Transfer this information, enlarging the drawing onto a canvas. Maintain the small background space. Look closely at individual details of lines, textures and patterns which make up the appearance of the animal. Practise mixing colours with your paints to match these areas as closely as possible. Experiment with different techniques to apply the paint to the canvas such as small dots of colour in the pointillist style or small thick brushstrokes. Remember that the direction of your brushwork is very important if you want to emphasise textures and patterns.

EDGAR PAU, student.

Creating wearable works using the animal theme

1 Create a piece of jewellery from any natural or man-made material, based on the theme of animals. The aim of this exercise is not to reproduce the animal realistically but to symbolise the animal's identity. Before making the jewellery write down the essential qualities of the animal. List its individual characteristics.

Example 1: leopard
- spots
- colours – gold and black
- fur
- sleek, graceful
- bright yellow/green eyes
- long tail

These components could be organised in any combination using a variety of materials.

Example 2: tropical fish
- transparent fins
- floats
- graceful
- brilliant colours
- shiny
- always moving
- lightweight

ROBYN GORDON, *Finch and Pardalote Ball,* 1984 neckpiece and earrings set, plastic and textile, Art Gallery of Western Australia. Courtesy of Crafts Council of Australia, The Rocks, Sydney.

ROBYN GORDON, three pairs of earrings from *A Snorkeller's Dream,* 1982 plastic, glass, shell and coral. Courtesy of Crafts Council of Australia, The Rocks, Sydney.

Think of your jewellery design as a wearable work of art or a mini-sculpture. It may be made up of abstract shapes and textures which suggest these qualities. Decide which part of the body the jewellery is designed for. Try to devise new ways of wearing jewellery.

2   Explore possibilities of manipulating natural fibre or found materials, which could include plastic tubing, handmade paper, cane reed, felt, wire, wire mesh, fly screen, ribbon beads, papier-mâché, twigs, feathers, coloured perspex or metal scraps.

ANGELA HOLMES, student.

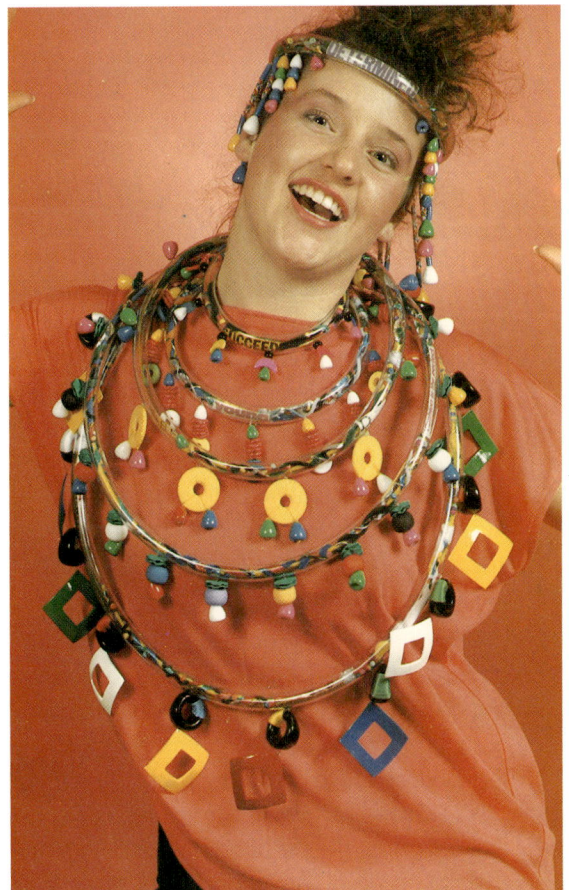

ANGELA HOLMES, student.

3   Record each stage in the development of your wearable, work from the preliminary sketches to the samples of materials chosen, including technical information about the actual construction of the piece.

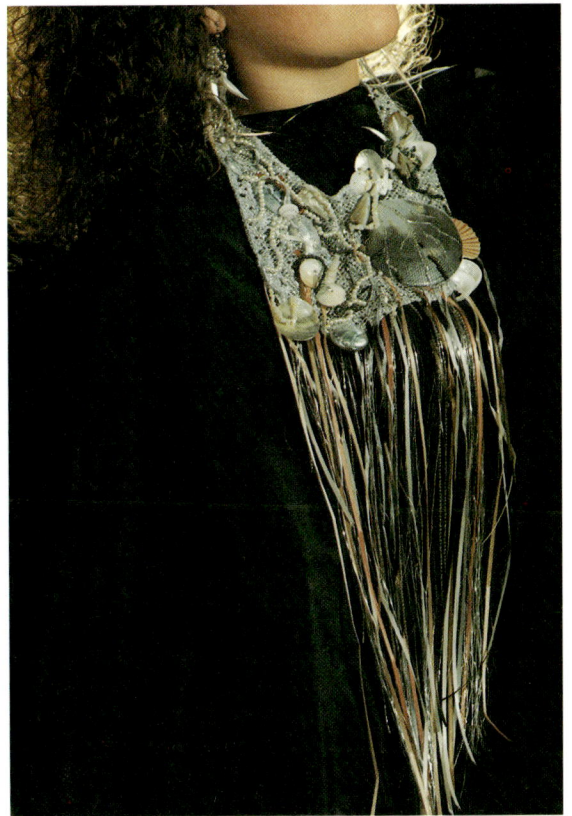

ANGELA HOLMES, student.

113

Silk screen designs based on primitive animal motifs

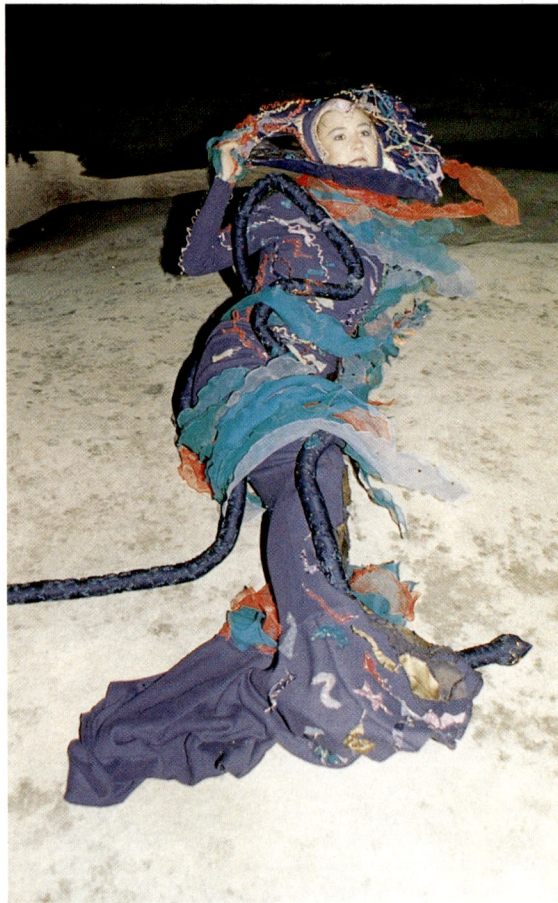

DANIELLE PARKER, student.

1 Look closely at paintings and carvings by Aboriginal artists or artists from other ancient cultures. Note the characteristics of their depiction of animals. Many of the animal forms are reduced to flat two-dimensional designs, showing the most important characteristic of the animal. Patterns and lines are a very important component of their work.

2 Create a design suitable for a silk-screen print on fabric, showing influence from these works. The design should be based on an Australian animal. (See section on simple silk-screen techniques). Develop your design to include four stencils for four colours. Your colour choices could include earthy natural Australian outback colours or bright vivid tropical or fluorescent colours. Print on to fabric, perhaps a T-shirt.

Design for a kimono based on animal theme

Experiment with a variety of fabric printing techniques: batik, tie-dyeing, crayon, dyes or fabric paint. Keep a collection of samples of your results which you can refer to whilst planning a design based on an animal or animals suitable for a simple kimono shaped garment. Base your design on the particular qualities of a particular animal or group of animals, for example, bird of paradise, tropical fish, an echidna. You may prefer to develop your printed techniques on scraps of calico or canvas. These could be used again directly onto the fabric of the kimono or cut out as pieces and sewn onto the garment (appliqué).

Linear definition could be achieved throughout the design by linking and overlapping with machine or hand stitching using dull or shiny threads. Scraps of coloured fabrics — shiny, rough, coloured cords or even tubing could be incorporated. Think of the finished garment as a work of art viewed from all angles, maintaining continuity in your design as it moves from front to back.

114

The Found Object

Food

1 Do a series of drawings of foods such as:
   (a) a crusty bread roll with sesame seeds and an interesting filling
   (b) a cross section of a vegetable or fruit with seeds, such as pumpkin, squash, tomato or capsicum
   (c) a thick wedge of cake with filling and icing
   (d) a product from the butcher such as T-bone steak, chops or brains
   (e) a bone
   Emphasise the shape and texture. Aim at detailed realism.

2 Create a large composition which combines several of the foods you have drawn. Use a variety of drawing materials such as pastels, conte crayons, cray-pas, charcoal or pitt pencils.

3 Experiment with some of the images you have drawn. Could they be stylised or transformed into other forms? Could the images assume other characteristics, for example, as forms in a surreal landscape? Using watercolours or inks and fine-point textas create a fantasy composition which incorporates transformations of your images.

SOHBI IBRAHIM, student.

4 Look at some of the artworks made by the Pop artist Claes Oldenburg. Analyse your food images. How could they be the starting point for a sculptural artwork (three-dimensional)? Consider a ceramic banquet using white clay and underglazes, or a giant-size soft sculpture created from canvas or other material.

5 Using your food images, design a poster to advertise a local supermarket or delicatessen. Remember, in advertising, images including lettering need to be simple, bold and clearly defined. Colours need to be fresh and pure. To be successful an advertisement needs to be easily identifiable and memorable.

Packages

1 Collect a variety of fast food packages and wrappers, eg Coke cans and bottles; McDonalds burger and chip cartons; Smiths Chips packets; Twisties packets; Chokito, Mars bars, Cherry Ripe wrappers; Popper cartons, etc.
   Experiment with squashing and crumpling some of the packages in slow motion, until you have decided which one would be the most interesting to draw.

2 Make a series of drawings to show changes in shape as the object is gradually squashed. Choose drawing materials that you think would be appropriate. If the package has lettering use it to emphasise the changing structure of the form.

3 Choose one product package. Create a silk-screen series based on the product along the lines of Andy Warhol's Campbell's Soup Cans.

4 Recreate a package in clay like Jasper Johns' Painted Bronze beer cans.

5 Using your collection of found packets and wrappers create a composition suitable for a painting. Consider where you would find these discarded wrappers – in and around garbage bins in a city street or shopping centre? Littering a beach or park? Piled up against a fence blown by the wind?
   Go out into the local environment with your sketchbook or camera to investigate possibilities for your painting. Sketch and/or photograph a number of different situations where rubbish is found. Evaluate the results. Organise the images in your composition to include some of your found packets and wrappers. Experiment with colour schemes and painting techniques before you start your composition.

6 Create a soft sculpture of the things from the garbage bin. Include painting, printing, batik, an appliqué texture to enhance the image.

CATHY FRANK, student.

TANYA WHEELER, student.

Classroom Experiences

Observation drawing

- pure contour drawing
- modified contour drawing
- realistic drawing

1 Look at simple found objects. List everyday objects which have interesting elements, such as shape, surface, texture or colour qualities. These could be organised into natural/man-made groups, for example:
    - natural — twigs, leaves, fruit, rocks (anything which is inanimate).
    - man-made — school bag, tap, clock, car parts, telephone, shoe, shirt, garlic press, cheese grater, a piece of machinery, television set, lipstick.

    Select one particular object of which you can provide a real example to work from.

THEO KOUSSIDIS, student.

2 Do a series of sketches of this object
    (a) from memory
    (b) looking only at the object, drawing without looking at the page
    (c) modify the previous drawing by adding detail from your direct observation of the object
    (d) from different viewpoints — above, sideways, below
    (e) draw with a selection of different mediums — thick graphite pencil, charcoal, crayon, watercolour pencil
    (f) wax resist drawing with wax and ink
    (g) pen and ink
    (h) paint, eg drawing with palette knife and paint, calligraphy brush
    (i) drawing emphasising lines using Artline texta

Magnified charcoal drawings

Extend one or a series of the drawings from the previous exercise as a magnified or extremely close up drawing of **part** of your object, for example, the buckle and strap on a school satchel. Emphasise textures and patterns, eg woven cloth; tones, eg shadows and highlighted areas; surfaces, eg shiny surfaces contrasting with dull matt surfaces.

Photographic portrait of still life subject

With careful attention to lighting take a photograph of your object from at least three interesting viewpoints. Develop and enlarge to 8 x 10 inch in the darkroom.

Photo-montage extension of found object

1 Select an unusual environment for your found object, for example, a school bag on the surface of the moon, or a lipstick standing amongst tall buildings. Cut out the photograph of your object and superimpose it into your new environment to create a fantasy dream-like scene. You may prefer to draw your object (as realistically as possible) and insert it into new scenery.

2 This experiment could be extended further by using mixed media — photographs, crayons, paints or collage materials.
    See works by Surrealists, naive artists, Rousseau and Chagall for ideas.

Distortion of found object image

1 Using one of your realistic drawings or photographs, cut the image into random strips or lengths or widths. Arrange on a sheet of art paper, varying the spaces between the strips.

2 Using lead pencil fill in the gaps as realistically as possible matching your pencil work with the corresponding section of the photograph. This should result in a realistic distortion of the original image in different tones of black and white.
    Look at the works of the Futurists, Cubists and Op painters for inspiration.

Abstract wax crayon design

1 Create a detailed wax crayon drawing of your object. Experiment with mixing colours and reproducing textures.

2 Create a second drawing using the same technique but from a different viewpoint.

3 Cut both drawings into strips or shapes of various sizes and recompose into a new **abstract** version of the original subject. Experiment with moving the strips and shapes up and down as well as sideways. Paste down on a coloured background, preferably cardboard.

Look at the works of the Analytical Cubists, and photography of David Hockney.

Sculptural experience in class groups using found objects

1 Select a range of inexpensive everyday objects such as drinking straws, plastic cups, string, plasticine. Organise this equipment into a number of equal kits.

2 Divide the class into equal groups of two to three students and give each group a sculpture kit. Ask each group to create a three-dimensional object/sculpture using the materials in the kit only. Stress the fact that the sculpture does not have to look like a realistic object, but may exist in its own right.

Experiment with manipulating the materials — cutting up, joining, suspending, building up. The sculpture may exist purely as an interesting structure or may move or function.

3 After a set time (approximately 20 minutes) reassemble and compare results. Discuss, exhibit and record observations.

Individual sculpture using assemblage technique and found objects

1 Create a three-dimensional or relief sculpture using a combination of materials and the assemblage technique. Consider the variety of materials available — old dolls, parts of cars, combs, plastic cups, combinations of junk, tyres, bicycle wheels, **or** use natural objects such as twigs, branches, leaves, shells or feathers.

2 Look at assembled sculptures of Pop artists — Keinholz, Claes Oldenburg, Duchamp, Paolozzi. Discuss possibilities of kinetic sculpture. Extend colour and surface with paint, glazing or lacquer.

Three-dimensional 'wrapped sculpture' experiment

1 Collect a range of interestingly shaped objects which are inexpensive or have been discarded. Using a variety of materials and strong glue, experiment with wrapping techniques which enhance the original form.

Materials which could be used may include: hessian, soft cane reed, cellophane, cotton lawn, canvas, calico, plastic, mod-rock, string, wire, barbed wire etc.

Use your imagination!

2 As an extension of this work, add colour to the finished work, depending on the surface — soft watercolour paint wash on canvas, thicker paint rubbed onto the surface of hessian picking up weave, or graphite shading.

Look at works by Christo, conceptual artists, happenings.

Silk-screen design

1 Observe the found object closely from a single viewpoint. Do a simple line drawing of the object. Include all identifiable characteristics. Create a repeat design based on this image.

2 Paint carefully in flat colour taking care with colour scheme and repetition of elements.

3 Extend this as a motif for a silk-screened design. Look at works by Andy Warhol for reference.

Interpreting found object as a three-dimensional clay sculpture

1 Using the real object as a model to work from, create a clay sculpture. Experiment with traditional building techniques and adapt to suit the basic shape of your object, for example, coil or slab construction ensures structure is sound, particularly for possible firing.

Remember to also use correct joining procedure.

2 Gradually build up smaller details by adapting a variety of building techniques and tools. Use either white or red clay. White clay may not necessarily be glazed at completion however it could be hand painted for subtle or very bright effects.

3 Extend your imagination by possibly choosing an object which is usually soft and yielding, such as a school satchel, soft sandshoe or folded clothing.

PART 3
DO IT YOURSELF

Lino Printing

Materials Required

- lino (usually obtainable in squares from most art suppliers)
- lino cutting tools (again available in packets of 6-12 tools)
- lino printing ink
- rubber rollers
- sheet of perspex or glass
- spatula
- rice paper or other suitably absorbent paper
- printing press (not absolutely necessary)

Lino printing requires direct carving with lino carving tools, into a sheet of lino. Similar results to wood block carving can be achieved, and most students find lino easier to handle. A variety of tools are available which can create different patterns on the surface of the lino.

Step 1

Using small pieces of spare lino or lino scraps, experiment on carving into the lino with the lino tools. At this stage do not attempt to create a picture, just interesting patterns of lines.

When carving, always remember to carve away from yourself, turning the lino gradually if necessary, rather than carving towards yourself which can prove very dangerous if you slip. You will also need to support the lino with your other hand whilst carving.

If the lino is difficult to cut into and feels brittle, simply heat gently with an iron or place near the classroom heater, then recommence.

Step 2

After experimenting with the carving tools look at your resulting patterns and textures. In a finished design these carved out areas would appear white after printing. (You may wish to print these experiments before continuing further. If so see printing instructions.)

Step 3

The nature of lino printing makes it more suitable to a semi-abstract or abstract design rather than a realistic scene for printing.

A simplified scene or abstract design will allow you to develop formal qualities such as shape, texture and pattern.

Consider also the size of your design, as this could be affected by the size of available lino.

Step 4

Possible themes suitable for lino block designs could include: animal forms — native fauna, marine creatures, bird life; faces — designs based on portraits of classmates with different expressions; objects — detailed designs based on magnified views of mechanical objects; or plants — native flora.

(a) Make a realistic sketch of the subject.
(b) Simplify your drawing into interesting shapes and lines. Magnify your viewpoint or re-arrange parts to create a semi-abstract or abstract design. You might allow straight or mainly curved lines to dominate the design depending on the subject. Whilst designing, imagine how some of the effects achieved in Step 1 could be applied to your design.
(c) Consider the positive and negative areas of your design. Where will these be. Make an extra copy of the design and shade in the areas you would like to see printed black or coloured and leave white those areas of pattern you would like to see carved out. Experiment with variations.

Step 5

When you are satisfied with your finished design, transfer it onto your lino with clear pencil drawing lines.

Step 6

Commence carving into the lino, taking care to check your original plan as you proceed. Remember that those areas which are carved away will not pick up the ink.

Step 7

To ink up the lino you will need to place a sheet of glass or perspex onto some sheets of newspaper. In the middle of the glass put about two teaspoonfuls of lino ink with the spatula or a spoon.

Using a rubber roller spread the ink evenly backwards and forwards and from side to side to create an area of ink about the same size as your sheet of lino.

Step 8

Have your sheets of paper ready beside the area where you are inking up the lino. Now you are ready to ink up. Roll the roller over the ink rolling in one direction only. Do this a few times until the ink is evenly coated on the roller. Now roll off onto the lino, rolling in one direction only until the lino appears evenly coated with ink. Take care with edges and corners as these must be coated evenly too.

Step 9

Carefully place your sheet of paper down onto the inked lino (with clean hands). At this stage you may wish to put the lino and paper through a press, or you can turn the lino over carefully and gently rub the back of the paper with your finger tips and then the smooth edge of a wooden spoon until the design appears to be printed evenly.

Step 10

Peel off the paper carefully and you should have an evenly transferred print. Allow to dry and observe results.

It may be necessary to do several prints before perfecting the required amount of ink. This will come with practice.

Make a Silk Screen Print

Silk screen printing is an art form in which many reproductions of the one print image can be produced. The process can be used to print onto many different surfaces such as paper, cardboard, fabric, ceramic, metal and even some plastics. In this process a stencil is attached to a mesh screen which is stapled tightly to a frame. Printing ink is then forced through the screen and stencil with a rubber bladed squeegee onto the printing surface.

The easiest type of stencil to use is a paper stencil. There are, however, many different materials which act as stencils or block outs on the screen available from art suppliers. There are several types of stencil film for handcut images. Some are attached to the screen using water, others with lacquer thinners or acetone. Also available is a type of stencil film on which can be registered a photographic image. Other materials such as gum acacia and litho crayons can be painted or drawn directly onto the screen for a more freehand calligraphic effect.

For beginners, it is advisable to start with simple one-colour paper stencils. As your confidence grows with this medium, further experimentation with multicolour prints and a variety of techniques will produce an exciting range of art images. In major works, silk screen printing can be combined with a variety of drawing and painting materials when printed onto paper, cardboard, canvas and other fabrics.

Simple One-Colour Printing

Draw up your design on art paper ensuring that no shapes touch or overlap. Make sure your design fits within the size of your screen.

Cut out the shapes using a stencil knife. The stencil knife is held like a pencil and achieves the cleanest edge if held at a 45 degree angle to the paper.

Tape your cut out stencil face down on the back of the screen, masking any uncovered areas around the edges of the mesh with paper.

Set up a printing area with a surface that is less resistant and hard than a table top. A felt mat or a flat wad of newspaper will serve the purpose.

Place the screen on top of the printing paper, ensuring that it is straight. Spoon a small quantity of printing ink along the top of the screen mesh.

The first print will require more printing ink as some is absorbed into the mesh and the stencil. If the screen is not hinged to a base board a classmate will need to hold the screen steady while you squeegee the ink down the screen, forcing the ink through the mesh and stencil onto the printing surface.

Hold the squeegee at approximately a 45 degree angle and drag the ink all the way to the bottom of the screen, pressing down slightly. If one drag is not sufficient to cover all the stencil, pick up the reserved ink with the squeegee and repeat the process. Make sure you only use the side of the squeegee blade which the ink is on.

Avoid unnecessary repetitions as this will only flood the stencil, causing leakages on the print.

Carefully lift the screen away from your print. Place the print in a drying rack or hang up to dry. Repeat the printing process for several copies (editions) of your print image.

Equipment Needed

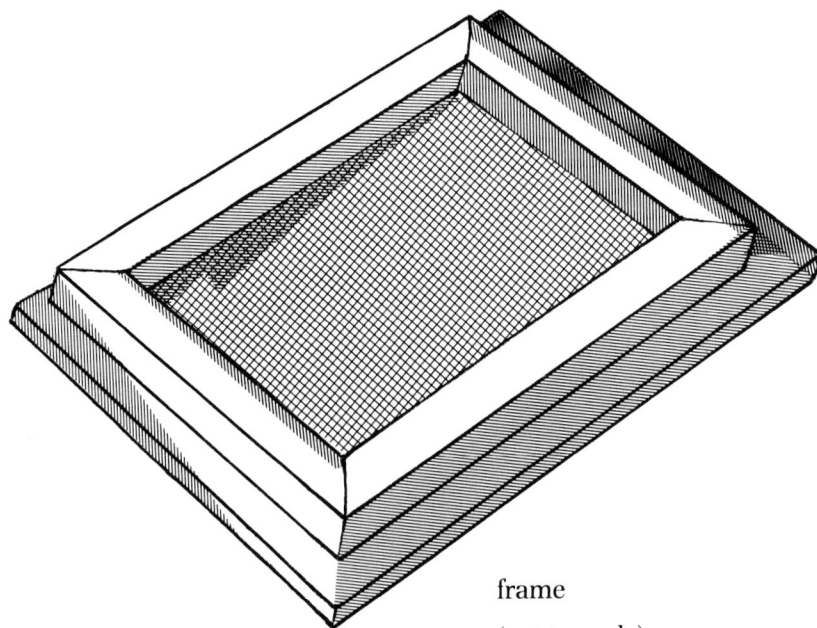

frame
(not to scale)

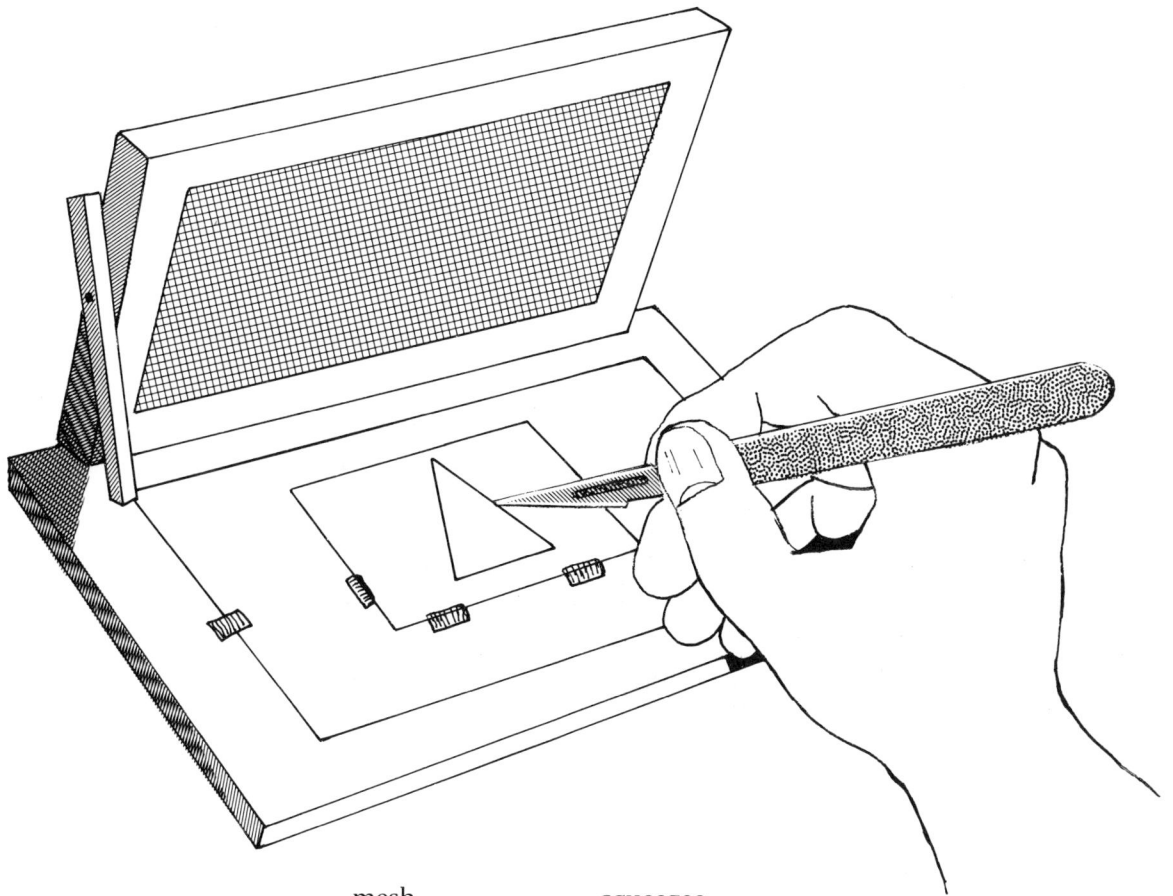

mesh

silk screen

stencil knife

wooden handle

rubber blade

squeegee
- masking tape
- art paper
- printing ink

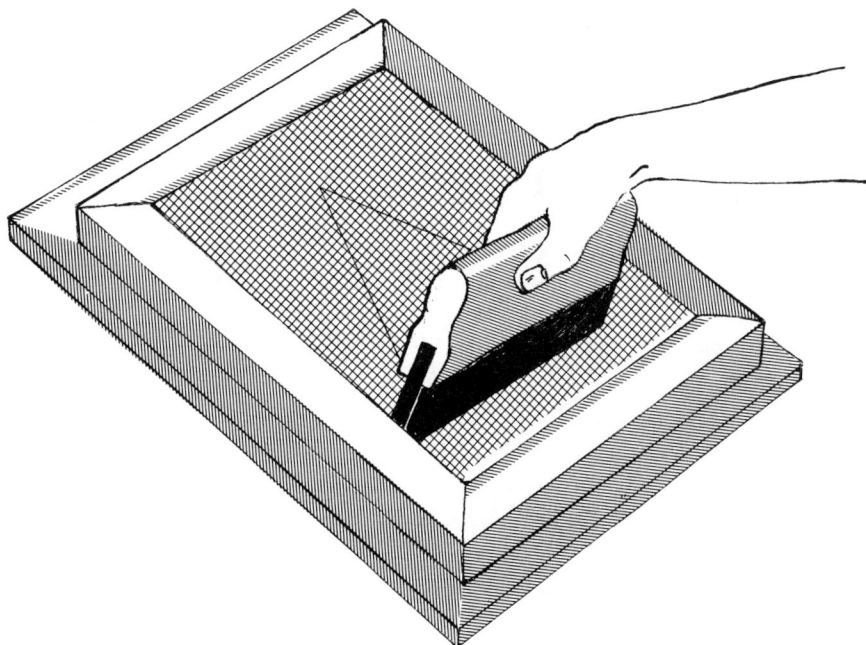

Build With Clay

Clay is a term used for rock which has decomposed and has become **plastic**. Plastic means that it is soft, malleable and can be manipulated with your hands to form a variety of shapes. As clay dries it becomes hard and retains its shape. If heat or fire is applied to clay it becomes stronger, more durable and rock-like.

There are many different hand building techniques which can be explored. Four of the most commonly used techniques are pinching, coiling, slabs and mould pots. Combinations of these techniques can be used to create an interesting array of pots and sculptural forms.

Pinch Forms

Bowls with feet
Small coils can be added to the base of pinch pots to form a foot.

SALLIE PORTNOY, bowl.
Courtesy of Crafts Council of Australia, The Rocks, Sydney.

Animal Forms
Simple joined forms that are spherical or ovoid can be turned into animal forms.

LORRAINE JENYNS, *Magnificent Monotreme: Echidna.*
Courtesy of Crafts Council of Australia, The Rocks, Sydney.

Features and limbs can be added to the basic form.

The exterior surface of coiled pots may be left with outside coils showing or joined in a textured pattern.

PHILIP LAKEMAN, ceramic sculpture.
Courtesy of Crafts Council of Australia.

COLLEEN POZZI, salt and copper glazed bowl.
Courtesy of Crafts Council of Australia, The Rocks, Sydney.

Coiled Forms

Large sculptural forms can be made using the coiling technique. Large forms need to be made in stages. Allow the lower section to firm in order to stand the overall weight of the clay. At the same time, however, keep the top edge damp with a moist cloth to ensure that the edge is ready for building on when the drying has progressed sufficiently.

HERBERT FLUGELMAN, Torso 1969.
Ceramic and plants.

ANNA COHN, *Lawncrawler II* 1972.
Clay. Collection of the artist.

The pot surfaces may be smoothed out using potters' tools and scrapers. A wooden paddle may be used to beat the clay walls into the desired profile.

GREG SUGDEN and MERRIE HAMILTON, *Fishtank*.
Courtesy of Crafts Council of Australia, The Rocks, Sydney.

Slab Forms

The construction of pots and ceramic sculptures from flat slabs of clay is one of the most popular handbuilding processes. Cardboard templates of the component parts can be used to determine the correct shape and size of your slabs. Slabs sometimes need to dry to almost leather hard stage before you begin construction as clay in its most plastic stage tends to flop and bend. The design and construction technique of your forms will determine whether this is necessary. Edges to be joined need to be roughened and moistened with slip. A coil of clay on the inside seam of the form will facilitate stronger joins.

LEONE RYAN, *Australian Bush Life*.
Courtesy of Crafts Council of Australia, The Rocks, Sydney.

HIROE SWEN, ceramic box.
Courtesy of Crafts Council of Australia, The Rocks, Sydney.

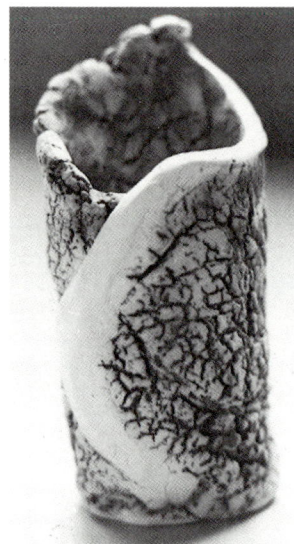

Slabs can be torn apart and the space filled with different coloured clays to create pattern.

Slabs can be rolled around carboard cylinders to create cylindrical forms.

Interesting textural patterns can be created by rolling clay slabs on textured surfaces such as hessian. Further pattern may be added using potters tools during the joining process.

Mould Pots

Moulds can be created from any container or carton such as icecream containers and milk cartons.

Plates and bowls can serve as moulds for other clay plates and bowls if they are lined first with plastic or material so the clay won't stick.

Clay mushroom cut-outs in white clay were arranged in the mould first, then coils of darker clay were positioned in the mould to complete the bowl form.

Interesting mould forms can be created by pressing a variety of clay shapes into the mould, such as round balls, and coils twisted into spirals.

Plaster moulds can be made in icecream containers, or cardboard boxes. Pour plaster into the mould, then use a greased shot-put to create a rounded void. Remove the shot-put when the plaster has set.

Forms can be extended beyond the mould with coils.

Slab boxes can be made by pressing clay inside a prepared cardboard box.

127

Make a Mask

Study primitive masks of Melanesia, Africa, North West Indians, Indonesia, Papua New Guinea; Ancient Greek Drama masks; Aboriginal and Papua New Guinean face make-up; and contemporary make-up.

Masks can be made to be worn from papier mâché or simply as art objects from clay.

Papier Mâché Masks

Here are two methods for making papier mâché masks.

1   Use heavy duty cardboard strips stapled together to make a frame. Paper strips (newspaper or telephone book paper) dipped in wall paper paste are then plastered over the frame in layers. Once dry, materials such as paint, foil, wool, hair, wire can be added to the basic form to create features. Holes can be cut into the masks for eyes and mouth if it is going to be worn.

2   Another method is to use a mould of some sort covered in plastic, on which the glue-dipped paper strips can be laid in layers. Facial features can be built up by taping down three-dimensional cardboard forms or scrunched pieces of paper then covered with further layers of papier mâché. Decorate the surface as in the first method.

Clay Masks

Clay masks are made by rolling out slabs of clay and cutting out the main shape, which can then be left as a flat slab or draped over a mould.

Features may be impressed, modelled, cut out, carved or applied to the clay shape to form the features and facial expressions.

After bisque firing, use oxides and glazes to enhance decorative features.

Primitive mask, wood, natural fibres and ochres. Papuan Gulf Province, Papua New Guinea. Pacific Collection, Australian Museum.

Making a Mobile

Unlike other types of sculpture, mobiles are not anchored to the ground or necessarily to a base. Mobiles are sculptures which can physically move, whether as the result of wind currents or by mechanical force.

Alexander Calder introduced wind mobiles in the 1930s and 1940s. These were made from plates of metal and a variety of other materials such as pieces of glass and wood suspended on strings and wires.

To create a mobile you will need to explore the processes of assemblage through experimentation with available materials. Materials which may be suitable for making mobiles could include:

- linear materials: cane reed, wire, thread, wool, raffia, string, pipe cleaner, twigs, rope.
- sheet materials: plastics, perspex, cellophane, masonite, cardboard, paper, foils, netting, gauze, nylon, flyscreen, mesh, sheet metal scraps.

Try using familiar objects in a new way.

Sources of Inspiration

Due to the physical nature and construction of mobiles it is not necessary to attempt a realistic subject but advisable to suggest the subject in a semi-abstract or abstract way.

Natural forms can be used as inspiration as it is possible to research certain structural components of the internal and external forms. Nature's designs can be inspirational, particularly insects which reveal their adaptation to their environment, stages of growth and development. A possible theme could be *A Fantasy Insect.*

The human form also holds possibilities for interior structure and external wrappings. Consider *Inside the Mind* as a possible theme for a mobile. When looking at a subject study it from all viewpoints looking at all its component parts. You may wish to recombine these different components into a new, imaginative assemblage of parts.

The mobile may be an imaginative exploration of materials assembled in unusual combinations, emphasising contrasting and harmonising physical qualities without being based on a particular subject.

Step 1

Consider the following concepts for inspiration:
(a) swinging (b) hovering (c) floating (d) spinning
(e) trapped   (f) fluttering

Step 2

Collect some suitable materials for construction of a mobile, such as cane or bamboo, fishing line, heavy cardboard, papier mâché, thin sheets of aluminium, clay forms and so on. Mobiles can be constructed from almost any material but it is essential that the supporting rods and wire are strong enough to carry the weight of the suspended forms. If your mobile is asymmetrical remember to balance your shapes on either side so that your mobile swings freely and doesn't tilt at a peculiar angle. Interesting abstract mobiles can be constructed from heavy white cardboard cut into organic shapes, painted on one side with a bright colour. Cut holes in the shapes, then twist and staple them so that they create three-dimensional forms. Suspend the forms by fishing line from small rods. As the mobile moves, the forms twist in space creating contrasts between colour and white, form and void.

Explore the possibilities of your chosen materials. Can you manipulate your materials in order to: coil, wind, loop, weave, draw with, join, flatten, bend, shape, curve, support other materials?

Step 3

Experiment with techniques of joining and assembling individual parts. Different techniques with varying materials will suggest certain concepts. The mobile form may be achieved by a repetition of moving units.

Step 4

When organising the component parts of the mobile consider:
(a) Advantages and disadvantages of the mobile form.
(b) Physical movement — affected by air currents.
(c) Weightless qualities — possible lightweight structure, transparent materials. Interior structure may be revealed.
(d) Effect of lighting — explore contrasts of surface, reflected light.

Experiment with combinations of line, negative space, positive space, colour and surface.

Step 5

When construction is completed, suspend in an airy environment, preferably outdoors or in strong light and evaluate the result. Observe the resulting spatial patterns, reflections and shadows.

Papermaking

Materials Required

- electric blender/kitchen whiz
- shredded computer paper – white or coloured
- large plastic trays
- kitchen sieve
- buckets
- chux/samples of a variety of fabrics with different textures
- newspaper
- press – wooden
- small plastic containers (ice cream)
- mould and deckle (see illustration)

Step 1

Make a mould and deckle from wood and fly-screen wire.

Step 2

Place a handful of shredded paper into your blender. Add water until the blender container is approximately three-quarters full. Blend until almost completely mashed to a milky consistency. Check the consistency by pouring out a little. Look for an even mixture without lumps of wet paper.

Transfer the blended pulp into bucket and continue to blend in small quantities as before. Keep transferring liquid until you have made approximately one bucketful of the mixture.

Step 3

Transfer the mixture into a deep plastic tray. Fill about half to three-quarters full.

Step 4

Carefully position mould and deckle at the edge of the tray. The mould is held flat with the wire mesh on top. On top of this, position the deckle and hold the two pieces together firmly. Agitate the mixture gently until even.

Lower the mould and deckle into the tray at the end closest to yourself. Gently slide along the bottom of the tray. Scoop upwards towards the back of the tray, allowing the mixture to gather in the mould.

Lift the mould and deckle straight up through the water, allowing the water to gradually drain out. Agitate gently until nearly all the water has gone and a soft damp mass of white pulp remains. Carefully remove the deckle from the top of the screen.

Step 5

Carefully take the screen over to a layer of dampened newspapers. Place a layer of cloth (eg cheesecloth or chux cloth) flat onto the pile of newspapers. Lower the frame towards the fabric and squeeze the wet pulp out of the screen onto the fabric, keeping the shape of the piece of paper. Cover with another cloth. Make as many sheets of paper as possible with the quantity of your mixture. Experiment using materials with different textures.

Step 6

When you have finished making paper, pack beneath a printing press and apply pressure for a couple of hours so as to squeeze out remaining water. Release the pressure of the press and carefully take out each sheet of paper as they were placed between the material samples.

Place flat to dry in the sun or dry with a hairdryer.

Step 7

Variations on white sheets of paper can be created with coloured shredded paper of reasonably good quality to maintain permanence of colour. Experiment with different combinations of coloured pulp.

Step 8

Collect a variety of natural plant forms, threads, dry leaves, grass. Put these into the paper pulp mixture in the large tray and scoop up with the mould and deckle. These specimens will create interesting textural effects when imbedded into the structure of the paper.

Making a Soapstone Sculpture

Themes to explore in soapstone

Due to the nature of soapstone carving, it is advisable to suggest a form rather than to try copying from life realistically. To a great extent the subject you will create in soapstone will depend on the size and shape of the original block. Simple organic forms are an excellent source of inspiration, ranging from animals to the human form. Themes such as growth and decay can also be expressed in abstract terms through carving.

When looking at aspects of the environment consider the following:
- shape relationships
- relationships of mass and space
- textural relationships
- qualities of mood and atmosphere

The process involved in carving is working on the **reduction** of your research to an essential form.

Inspiration

For inspiration when developing ideas for soapstone sculptures, look closely at the sculptures of Jean Arp, Henry Moore, Barbara Hepworth and Constantin Brancusi. These sculptors have all shown a sensitivity to natural forms and materials through their development of organic sculptures.

Jean Arp (1887-1966) experimented early in his career with painted relief sculptures but by the 1930s he turned to sculpture in the round. His work is in bronze (from clay and plaster models) and marble. He emphasised mass rather than space and his forms have been called Biomorphic.

Arp was a lover of peace and nature; a gentle man. Arp's work represents the essence of life itself — organic growth both in humans and in nature.

Find the words which best describe Arp's sculptural forms; sharp, harsh, organic, angular, abstract, jagged, geometric, undulating, fluid, realistic, flowing, curving or soft.

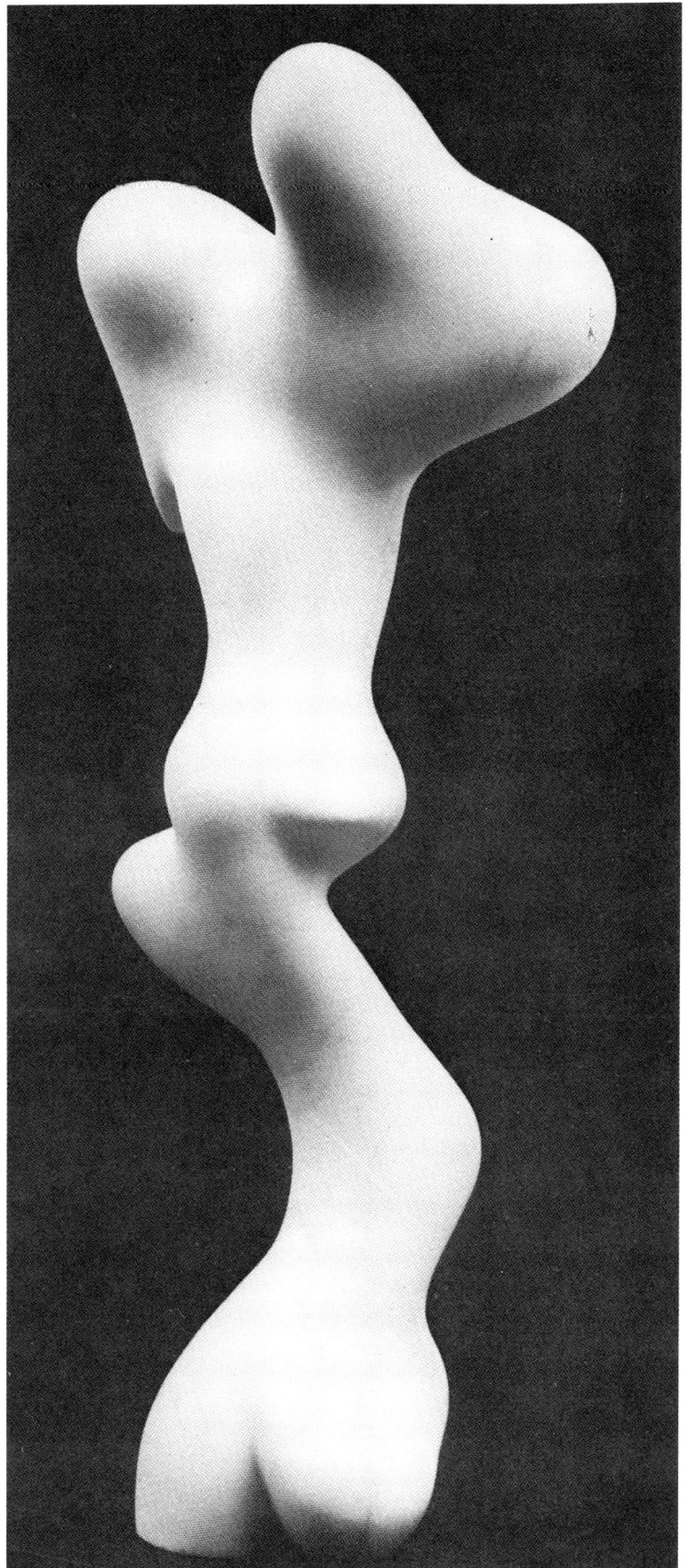

JEAN (HANS) ARP, Growth (Croissance), 1938. (opposite)
Marble, height 100.33 cm.
Collection: Solomon R Guggenheim Museum, New York.

Step 1

When you have been issued with your soapstone, make decisions about subject matter. Look at the piece of stone – do experimental research drawings which simplify, eliminate, reduce, exaggerate and elongate. The quality of soapstone usually suggests simplistic forms with smooth, curved, undulating surfaces. Consider the technique of carving – reducing from a solid block. Consider the natural characteristics of the stone – the shape, natural patterns, colour variations and faults which occur when developing your sculptural ideas.

Step 2

Using a file or rasp remove rough edges of stone and streamline into general shape of your planned drawing.

Step 3

Make decisions now on negative spaces. Create holes in the rock using a hand drill. Now enlarge these with a small file, opening the hole outwards towards you. Continue to use the heavier files and rasps until the overall shape starts to resemble your sketch. Work with the stone rather than against it. Make modifications. As you work look at your sculpture. Evaluate it. It is taking on a living, organic form? Is it interesting from all angles? Is the surface pleasing to touch? Try making some parts rough and some parts smooth if it suits your form.

Step 4

Use a coarse grade of sandpaper to eliminate tool marks (if desired) and soften curves and edges of holes. Continue to sand the sculpture using finer grade papers until a very smooth finish is achieved.

Step 5

To develop an even smoother finish, it will now be necessary to rub the surface of your sculpture vigorously with a **cutting compound** which can be obtained from the soapstone supplier. This compound will gradually remove the fine lines left by the sandpaper.

Step 6

Rub the surface vigorously again, this time with a **polishing compound.** Continue rubbing until the sculpture looks and feels extremely smooth.

Step 7

The final stage requires the application of a **polishing wax.** Take care to cover the entire surface evenly then buff off vigorously with a soft cloth. Continue polishing until the waxy film has been completely removed and the sculpture no longer feels greasy.

Step 8

Evaluate and admire the finished result.

JEAN (HANS) ARP, *Mythical Sculpture* 1949.
Limestone, height 64.77 cm. Courtesy Weintraub Gallery, New York.

Develop and Print Black and White Photographs

Equipment You Will Need

The Darkroom

To set up a darkroom you will need a room that can be totally blacked out. It is preferable to choose a room with as few window and door openings as possible to minimise the possibility of light leakage into the darkroom. Windows can be blacked out by painting them with a couple of layers of matt black paint then covering them with a blind or curtain. Light leakages under and around doors can be prevented by hanging a curtain of black material across the door. However, it is also essential to have a ventilation system such as an extraction fan to draw off chemical fumes.

The darkroom should have a dry bench area where the enlarger is set up. All items that must be kept dry such as photographic paper, negative holders and enlarging meters, should be kept on shelves or in drawers in this area. You will need power outlets in the dry bench area for the enlarger, safelights and other electrical equipment.

A wet bench area is set up near a sink. In this area developing tanks and developing trays are set out and mixing of chemicals takes place.

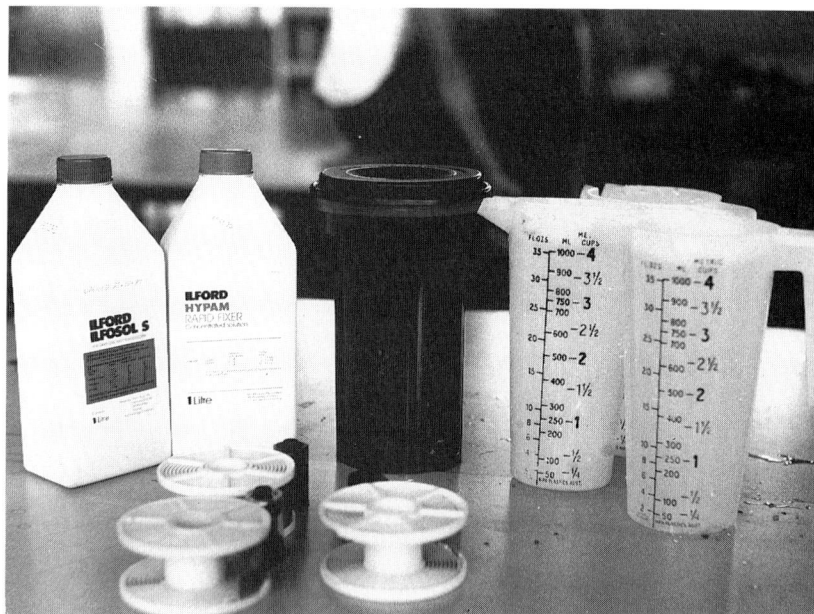

Developing Film

The following equipment is needed.
- **developing tank**
- **developing spool** (spiral)
- **three measuring cylinders** (or jugs)
- **scissors**
- **film developer** (eg Ilford Ilfosol finegrain film developer)
- **film fixer** (eg Ilford Hypam rapid fixer)
- **wetting agent**
- **change bag** (so that you can develop film out of the darkroom)

To develop film, it must be wound onto a developing spool (spiral) then placed in a developing tank for treatment with chemical solutions. This procedure must be carried out in total darkness because film is sensitive to all light including red/orange safe lights. If the darkroom is in use this step can be done using a change bag.

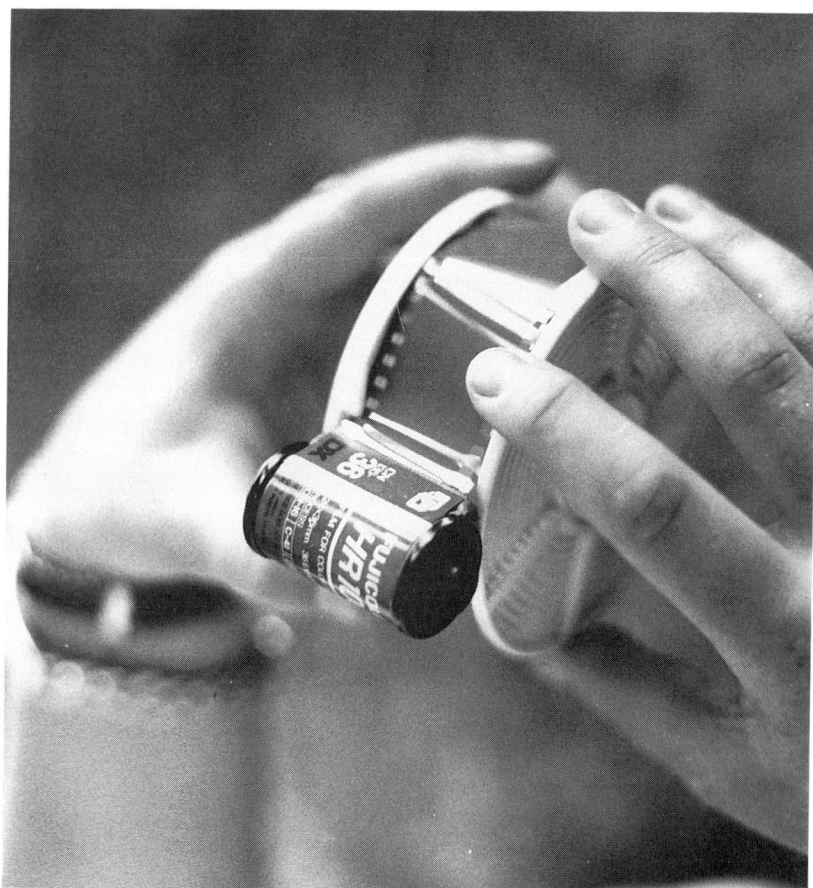

If the tongue of the film protrudes from the jaws of the cassette, gently pull it out a little and trim the film off square with scissors. This first step can be done with the light switched on. If the film is rewound completely into the cassette, the cassette must be opened and the film removed and cut in complete darkness. Most film cassettes have ends that pop off easily if pressure is applied to the protruding end on the desk top. Feed the end of the film into the entry slots of the spiral. Now the lights must be turned off. Pull the film out of the cassette and hold the spiral with both hands. Using a back and forth action, rotate each half of the spiral alternately so that the film is wound into the spiral. When the whole film is wound on cut off the end of the film to free it from the cassette, place the spiral into the developing tank and put the lid on. These tanks are light-tight but have a system by which chemicals can be poured into the tank through an opening in the lid.

Prepare your developer and fixer according to dilution instructions on the containers. The chemicals should be at 20° C. Development time will vary depending on the film used and the brand of developer. You will need to agitate the developing tank (by slow inversion) for 10 seconds, every minute. Pour out developer, pour in stop bath (fresh water will do) rinse well, then pour in prepared fixer solution. Use same agitation procedures as before for the specified time. Now pour out fixer and place tank under running water for 15 minutes. Turn off the tap. Add a small dribble of wetting agent (dishwashing detergent will do) into the developing tank and swirl it around. Remove the film negatives from the spiral and hang up to dry in a dust free environment.

Contact Printing and Enlarging Prints

The following equipment is needed.

- **enlarger**
- **timer**
- **enlarging meter** (to determine correct exposure time)
- **safelights** (red or orange)
- **contact printer**
- **masking easel**
- **three plastic developing trays**
- **three measuring cylinders**
- **thermometer**
- **paper developer** (eg Ilford paper developer)
- **paper fixer** (eg Ilford paper fixer)
- **photographic paper** (available in grades 1-5 or multigrade)

- **multigrade filters** (only if using multigrade paper)

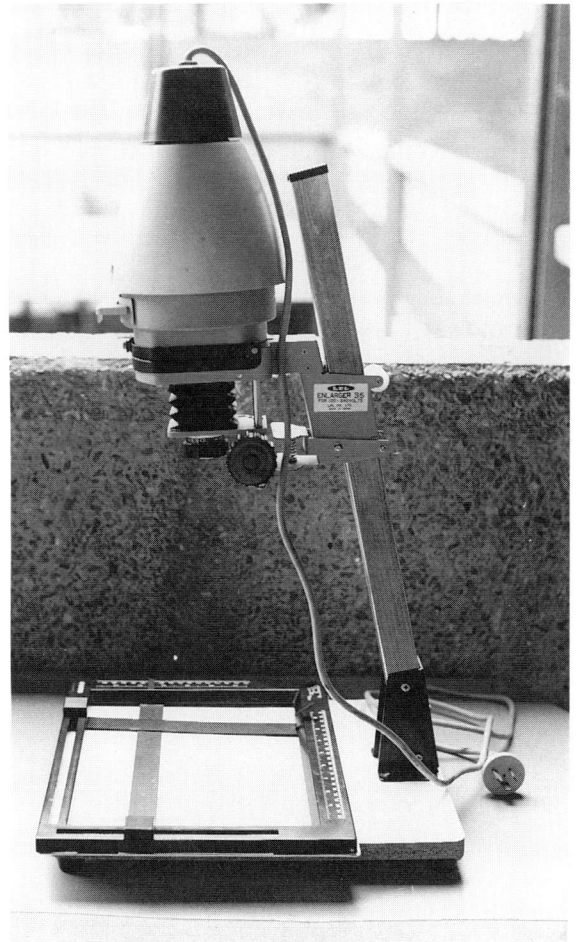

Contact Prints

Cut film negatives into strips of five or six frames. Place in contact printer with the **emulsion** side (dull side) facing towards the base of the printer. The emulsion side of the negatives will then be in **contact** with the photographic paper when it is exposed.

Mix up your chemicals before you switch off the main lights. Approximately 500 mls of prepared solution will sufficiently cover the bottom of each tray.

Follow dilution instructions on the containers. Ensure that the solutions are at approx. 20° C. Set out three trays for the following:
- developer
- stop bath (fresh water will do)
- fixer

Fill a larger tote tray with water in the sink.

Now you are ready to start printing. Turn off the main lights and turn on your safe lights, exhaust fan and the enlarger. You should have a safelight over the enlarger area and another over the wet area where the trays are set out.

Place the contact printer (with your negatives) on the baseboard of the enlarger. Raise the height adjustment of the enlarger to full height. Open the lens aperture to its widest setting (most light) and adjust the focus knob so that the light projected through the lens completely covers the contact printer. Set the timer to four or five seconds.

Now turn **off** the enlarger light before you take out any photographic paper. Remember photographic paper is sensitive to **all** light except red/orange light.

Take out a sheet of 8" x 10" Grade 3 paper. Place in contact printer. Start timer. The timer will automatically switch off at the time set. Now proceed with developing.

Slide paper into developing tray ensuring that all of the paper is covered immediately. Gently rock the tray so that the developing solution washes back and forth over the paper. Develop for 60 seconds.

Next place paper into stop bath (water). Wash using same rocking action for five seconds.

Now into the fixer using same action as above for 30 seconds. Prints must then be washed in fresh running water for at least five minutes before you take them out to dry.

Making Enlargements

Look at your contact print. Choose which photo you wish to print. Find the correct negative.

Place negative in the negative carrier of the enlarger with emulsion side (dull side) facing down.

Adjusts the height of the enlarger head for your size paper (eg 4 inch x 5 inch is lower down, 8 inch x 10 inch higher up).

Focus your image. It helps to have the lens aperture on full light when you focus.

Now you need to determine what exposure time is correct for your negative. Set the aperture on the lens to an average setting of approximately f. 5.6 or f. 8. Turn off the enlarger light before you take out a small strip of photographic paper. You are going to expose this test strip to three different exposure times, five, 10 and 15 seconds. Use a piece of cardboard to cover one-third of the test strip after five seconds and then two-thirds of the test strip after 10 seconds. Watch the timer care-

fully so you are accurate while the paper is being exposed.

If you have an enlarging meter to test exposure you will not have to do test strips. Read the instructions that come with it for the correct procedure.

Now process your test strip using the chemicals solution you have already set out.

Look at the test strip and decide which exposure time looks the correct. You may decide that perhaps 10 seconds is too light and 15 seconds too dark so choose a time between the two (eg 12 seconds).

Set the timer on the correct time. Now proceed with exposure and processing of your print enlargement. Negatives which look similar will usually have the same exposure time if the aperture is set on the same setting. So record the f. stop and exposure time for future reference.

Negatives which are more dense (darker) will require longer times or wider apertures (more light).

You must test all negatives that look significantly different in density. You must also remember to refocus each time you put a different negative into the enlarger.

Good luck and have fun!

Etching

Etching is an age old technique of reproduction, and is now recognised as an artform in its own right. It is used in order to achieve compositions rich in tone, from velvety blacks through subtle shades of grey to stark white. When a drawing is etched, greater dramatic effect can be achieved from the lines and textures.

Materials and Tools for Drypoint

- pre-soaked printing paper
- copper plate (zinc or plastic may also be used, but copper lasts longer)
- drypoint needle (a nail fitted into a handle is sufficient for beginners). Any tool capable of scratching the surface may be used, but the deeper the mark the better, because the lines will gradually wear away as the plate is passed through the etching press.
- ink dabber (a thick piece of cardboard is often used for this)
- oil-based printing ink
- etching press
- newspaper
- blotting paper
- soft cloth (gauze or similar)

Step 1

It may be desirable to commence with a drawing of your subject. This may then be copied onto the plate with the drypoint needle. Sometimes, however, fine spontaneous work is achieved by working directly onto the plate without preliminary sketches.

Step 2

Commence engraving the information from your original onto the drypoint plate or plastic sheet. This is done by carefully scratching the surface with a needle or other pointed tool. Experiment with the types of marks you can create — fine delicate lines, dots, thick, broad lines, deep or shallow lines. When using drypoint paper, variations of tone can be created by varying the depth of the cuts and scratches. The surface of the paper can be stripped in layers.

Step 3

Look closely at the engraved work. Take care with detail. Have you explored possibilities of tonal variation? Have you extended your original drawing due to the nature of the drypoint paper or plastic?

It is advisable to prepare the printing paper now. Do this by quickly dipping the paper in water. This will soften the paper. Then arrange the sheets of printing paper in layers between blotting paper or newspaper to soak up the excess moisture.

Step 4

Using the ink dabber or card, apply the oil-based printing ink evenly over the whole surface. When covered, wipe the surface with the gauze, taking care to ensure that the ink penetrates all the scratches and marks you have made on the surface of the plate. Then, take a piece of newspaper, (or better still, the pages of an old telephone book) and lightly rub over the whole surface to pick up any excess ink.

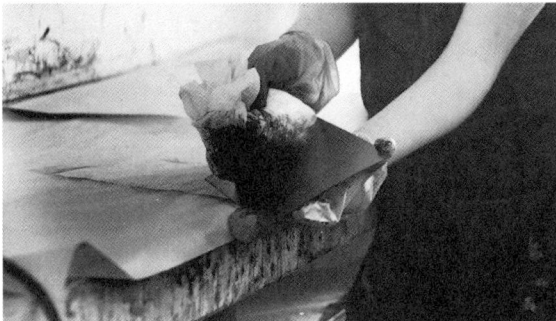

Step 5

Prepare the etching press by adjusting the pressure. Place a clean sheet of paper the same size as your printing paper on the steel bed of the press. Next, place the engraved plate face upward onto the paper. Carefully put the dampened printing paper on top of the plate. Place a felt blanket on top of the printing paper.

Step 6

Slowly turn the wheel of the press without stopping. Ideally this should be done only once, in one direction. Carefully remove the layers of paper from the press. The result should be a clear intaglio print.

Note: Drypoint is the simplest of the etching processes. More commonly, a thin film of **ground** (a compound resembling tar which resists acid) is applied to the surface of the plate. The ground is then marked or impressed with various tools, such as scrapers, burnishers or scribers. The plate, with the inscribed ground on its surface is then submerged in a solution of water and nitric acid. The acid eats through the marks in the same way as the drypoint needle penetrates the surface. Many and varied effects can be achieved. After this the plate is inked up and printed.

For Louise Katz, (seen at work in the photographs) the medium of etching provides scope for imagery suggestive of the past, of history.

LOUISE KATZ, *Hermaphrodite* 1986.
Etching.

138

PART 4
UNDERSTANDING
WORKS
OF
ART

Looking at Painting

Consider the following when analysing paintings:

The artist's philosophy – what is the artist aiming to do here?

Subject matter – is the painting depicting a religious theme, or perhaps bourgeois life in Paris in the 1890s, or a vision from the artist's imagination?

Colours – What colours are used? Is colour used to heighten the expressive quality of the painting? Is the colour used realistic? Is the colour restricted?

Line – Is it used to create an outline? To suggest energy, movement or emotion. To create a three-dimensional form?

Shape – Are the shapes used flat, solid, definite or indefinite?

Tones – Are there strong tonal contrasts or is the composition mainly light or dark?

Artist's interpretation of space – Is it limited or does the viewer experience a vast open panorama of space?

Use of light – Is it coming from a definite source? Is it of importance to the particular painting?

Mood – The way the painting makes you feel, eg. a tense, mysterious mood, bold and active or perhaps tranquil and relaxing.

Relationship between the viewer and the painting – Does the viewer feel drawn into the painting and involved with the subject?

Composition – What makes the painting hang together? Is it balanced? How has the artist organised the elements?

Technique – How has the painter actually applied the paint? Have short fleeting brushstrokes been used or has paint been squeezed straight from the tube and perhaps applied with the palette knife?

The following points should be considered when looking at individual artworks in painting.
- types of artistic expression
- effects of art styles on the viewer
- effect of the environment on the painter
- use of symbols and origins of art.

Values which can be applied when appreciating a painting.

1 Use values – **function:** What was the purpose of the work? Was it intended to be ceremonial, decorative, applied art, religious, satirical or social comment? Is it a personal expression? Consider the interaction of a personality with the culture.

2 Associated values – **themes:** What is the artist saying? The effect the work has on the viewer. The underlying philosophy, for example, the female image, images of gods.

3 Formal values – **elements, principles, composition techniques, media:** The way in which the artist manipulates lines, colours and form to get his/her message across.

140

Looking at Sculpture

These points should be used in analysis of individual works and in any type of essay on sculpture.

Period/style   When?

Sculptor   Who?

Title   . . .

Materials   What is it made of?
Clay, stone, plaster, plastic?
Natural or synthetic?

Method/processes How is it made?
Carved, modelled, cast,
assembled? What is the
process? Additive or
subtractive?

Function/purpose Why was it made?
For **religious** purposes? eg: to
decorate a church?
For **social** purposes? eg: make
comment on social problems?
For purely **aesthetic** purposes?
eg: artist concerned with pure
form, movement etc.
For **emotional** purposes?
Artist expressing his feelings.

Location/context   Where is it found?
Presentation   On a church?
In a shrine?
In a park?
In a gallery?
How is it presented?
On a building?
On a wall?
Flat on the ground?
On a pedestal?

Type of sculpture What type of sculpture is it?
Relief, free-standing, mobile?

Visual   Examine and analyse the
characteristics   sculptor's use of the **elements:**
mass, space, plane, line,
texture, colour, light.

Style   Examine and analyse the
characteristics   sculptor's approach to his
subject/theme.

Ask yourself is it — • realistic/naturalistic?
• idealistic?
• symbolic?
• expressive?
• distorted, simplified, exaggerated?

• abstract?
• semi-abstract?
• static/passive?
• kinetic (actually moves —
motorised, by wind through
space)?
• active (appears to move
through space)?

Index to Artists

Index to Artworks

Index to Student Works

(All student works not individually credited were contributed by students from Belmore Boys High School, Lurnea High School and Port Hacking High School.)

Australian Galleries

ACT

Australian National Gallery
Parkes, Canberra, Parkes Place, 2600
Contact Education Officer
Tel: (062) 71 2411

Australian War Memorial
Anzac Parade, Canberra, 2600
Tel: (062) 43 4211

Arts Council of Australia Gallery
Gorman House, Ainslie Avenue, Braddon, 2601
Tel: (062) 48 9813

Canberra School of Art Gallery
Baldessin Crescent, Canberra, 2601
Tel: (062) 46 7946

National Library of Australia
Parkes, Canberra, Parkes Place, 2600
Tel: (062) 62 1111

Nolan Gallery
Tharwa Drive, Lanyon, 2620
Tel: (062) 37 5192

Parliament House
Parkes, Canberra, 2600
Tel: (062) 72 1211

NEW SOUTH WALES

Albury Regional Art Centre
Dean Street, Albury, 2640
Tel: (062) 21 6384

Art Directors Gallery
21 Nurses Walk, The Rocks, 2000
Tel: (02) 27 2740

Art Gallery of New South Wales
Art Gallery Road, Sydney, 2000
Contact Education Officer
Tel: (02) 225 1700

Bathurst Regional Art Gallery
City Council Chambers, Bathurst, 2795
Tel: (063) 31 1622

Bega Valley Shire Council
Zingel Place, Bega, 2550
Tel: (0649) 2 1088

Broken Hill City Art Gallery
Chloride Street, Broken Hill, 2880
Tel: (080) 6602

Dubbo City Council
Church Street, Dubbo, 2830
Tel: (068) 82 2211

Dixson Gallery and Library
State Library of New South Wales
Macquarie Street, Sydney, 2000
Tel: (02) 230 1500

S H Ervin Art Gallery
Observatory Hill, Sydney, 2000
Tel: (02) 27 5374

Coffs Harbour Shire Council
Cnr Coff & Castle Streets, Coffs Harbour, 2450
Tel: (066) 52 2555

Gosford City Art Collection
Gosford City Council Chambers, Gosford, 2250
Tel: (043) 24 2811

Goulburn Regional Art Gallery
Sloane Street, Goulburn, 2580
Tel: (048) 21 1444

Grafton City Council
2 Prince Street, Grafton, 2460
Tel: (066) 42 2266

Griffith Regional Art Gallery
167-185 Banna Avenue, Griffith, 2680
Tel: (069) 62 5991

Ivan Dougherty Gallery
Sydney College of Advanced Education
Cnr Albion Avenue & Selwyn Street,
Paddington, 2021
Tel: (02) 339 9555

Lake Macquarie Community Art Centre Gallery
Old Council Chambers, Boolaroo, 2284
Tel: (049) 58 0459, (049) 58 5333

Lewers Bequest and Penrith Regional Art Gallery
86 River Road, Emu Plains, 2750
Tel: (047) 35 1448

Lismore Regional Art Gallery
Molesworth Street, Lismore, 2480
Tel: (066) 21 1536

Maitland City Art Gallery
Brough House, Church Street, Maitland, 2320
Tel: (049) 33 1657

Manly Art Gallery
West Esplanade, Manly, 2095
Tel: (02) 949 2435

Mint & Hyde Park Barracks
Queens Square, Macquarie Street, Sydney, 2000
Tel: (02) 217 0111

Muswellbrook Regional Art Gallery
Bridge Street, Muswellbrook, 2333
Tel: (065) 43 3984

New England Regional Art Museum
Kentucky Street, Armidale, 2350
Tel: (067) 72 5255

Newcastle Regional Art Gallery
Laman Street, Newcastle, 2300
Tel: (049) 293 263

Norman Lindsay Gallery and Museum
128 Chapman Parade, Faulconbridge, 2776
Tel: (047) 51 1067

Orange Regional Gallery
Byng Street, Orange, 2800
Tel: (063) 62 1555

Port Stephens Society of the Arts
Cultural Centre, Shoal Bay Road, Nelson Bay,
2315
Tel: (049) 81 3604

Power Gallery of Contemporary Art
University of Sydney, 2006
Tel: (02) 692 3170

Pro Hart Gallery
24 Bromide Street, Broken Hill, 2880
Tel: (080) 2441

Roslyn Oxley 9 Gallery
13 Macdonald Street, Paddington, 2021
Tel: (02) 331 1919

Shoalhaven City Council
Bridge Road, Nowra, 2540
Tel: (044) 21 6011

Taree Municipal Council Art Collection
Taree Municipal Council, Pulteney Street,
Taree, 2430
Tel: (065) 52 1126

Wagga Wagga City Art Gallery
Gurwood Street, Wagga Wagga, 2650
Tel: (069) 21 3621

Wollongong City Art Gallery
Cnr Keira and Burelli Streets, Wollongong East,
2500
Tel: (042) 28 7802

NORTHERN TERRITORY

Northern Territory Museum of Arts and Sciences
Bullocky Point, Darwin, 5790
Tel: (089) 82 4211

Museums & Art Galleries of Northern Territory
Star Village, Smith Street Mall,
Darwin, 5794
Tel: (089) 81 6488

Araluen Arts & Cultural Trust
Larapinta Drive, Alice Springs, 5750
Tel: (089) 52 5022

QUEENSLAND

Brisbane City Civic Art Gallery & Museum
City Hall, Brisbane, 4000
Tel: (07) 221 1507

Bundaberg Art Collection
Bourbong Street, Bundaberg, 4670
Tel: (071) 72 3700

Civic Art Gallery and Museum
Town Hall, King George Square, Brisbane, 4000
Tel: (07) 225 4355

The Gold Coast Collection
The Centre, 135 Bundall Road, Surfers
Paradise, 4217
Tel: (075) 31 9521

Institute of Modern Art
106 Edward Street, Brisbane, 4000
Tel: (07) 229 5985

Museum of Contemporary Art
Melbourne Street, South Brisbane, 4101
Tel: (07) 846 2255

Perc Tucker Regional Gallery
Flinders Mall, Townsville, 4810
Tel: (077) 72 2560

Queensland Art Gallery
Queensland Cultural Centre,
South Bank, South Brisbane, 4101
Contact Education Officer
Tel: (07) 840 7333

Queensland College of Art
Foxton Street, Morningside, 4170
Tel: (07) 395 9100

Rockhampton Art Gallery
City Hall, Victoria Parade, Rockhampton, 4700
Tel: (079) 27 7129

Toowoomba City Art Gallery
Ruthven Street, Toowoomba, 4350
Tel: (076) 379 5500

University Art Museum
University of Queensland
St Lucia, 4067
Tel: (07) 377 1111

SOUTH AUSTRALIA

Art Gallery of South Australia
North Terrace, Adelaide, 5000
Contact Education Officer
Tel: (08) 223 7200

Contemporary Art Society of Australia
14 Porter Street, Parkside, 5063
Tel: (08) 272 2682

The Flinders University Art Museum
Flinders University, Sturt Road,
Bedford Park, 5042
Tel: (08) 275 2695

Riddoch Art Gallery
Civic Centre,
Commercial Street East, Mt Gambier, 5290
Tel: (087) 24 1752

TASMANIA

Burnie Art Gallery
Wilmot Street, Burnie, 7320
Tel: (004) 31 5918

Devonport Gallery
Steel Street, Devonport, 7310
Tel: (004) 24 0561

Queen Victoria Museum and Art Gallery
Wellington Street, Launceston, 7250
Tel: (003) 31 6777

Tasmanian Museum and Art Gallery
5 Argyle Street, Hobart, 7000
Contact Education Officer
Tel: (002) 23 1422

Tasmanian School of Art Gallery
Olinda Street, Mount Nelson, 7007

Tel: (002) 20 3133

VICTORIA

Ararat Gallery
Town Hall, Vincent Street, Ararat, 3377
Tel: (053) 52 2836

City of Ballarat Fine Art Gallery
40 Lidyard Street, North Ballarat, 3350
Tel: (053) 31 5622

Banyule Gallery
60 Buckingham Drive, Heidelberg, 3084
Tel: (03) 62 7411

Benalla Art Gallery
Bridge Street, Benalla, 3672
Tel: (057) 62 3027

Bendigo Art Gallery
View Street, Bendigo, 3550
Tel: (054) 43 4991

Castlemaine Art Gallery and Historical Museum
Lyttleton Street, Castlemaine, 3450
Tel: (054) 72 2292

Caulfield Arts Centre
441 Inkerman Road, Caulfield, 3161
Tel: (03) 524 3277

Exhibition Gallery
Monash University, Wellington Road, Clayton, 3168
Tel: (03) 669 8666

Geelong Art Gallery
Little Malop Street, Geelong, 3220
Tel: (052) 93645

Gertrude Street Artist Spaces Inc
188 Gertrude Street, Fitzroy, 3065
Tel: (03) 419 3406

Grainger Museum
University of Melbourne, Parkville, 3052
Tel: (03) 344 5270

City of Hamilton Art Gallery
Brown Street, Hamilton, 3300
Tel: (055) 73 0460

Heide Park and Art Gallery
Templestowe Road, Bulleen, 3105
Tel: (03) 850 1849

City of Horsham Regional Art Gallery
Town Hall Building, 80 Wilson Street, Horsham, 3400
Tel: (053) 82 5575

City of St Kilda Art Collection
Town Hall, Brighton Road, St Kilda, 3182
Tel: (03) 536 1333

Latrobe Valley Arts Centre
138 Commercial Road, Morwell, 3840
Tel: (051) 34 1364

McClelland Gallery
McClelland Drive, Langwarrin, 3910
Tel: (03) 789 1671

Mildura Arts Centre
199 Cureton Avenue, Mildura, 3500
Tel: (050) 23 3733

Mornington Peninsula Arts Centre
4 Vancouver Street, Mornington, 3931
Tel: (059) 75 4395

National Gallery of Victoria
180 St Kilda Road, Melbourne, 3004
Contact Education Officer
Tel: (03) 618 0222

Performing Arts Museum
Victoria Arts Centre, 100 St Kilda Road, Melbourne, 3004
Tel: (03) 617 8211

Print Council of Australia
105 Collins Street, Melbourne, 3000
Tel: (03) 654 2460

RMIT Faculty Gallery
Building 2, 342-348 Swanston Street, Melbourne, 3000
Tel: (03) 662 0611

Sale Regional Arts Centre
Civic Centre, Macalister Street, Sale, 3850
Tel: (051) 44 2829

Shepparton Art Gallery
Civic Centre, Welsford Street, Shepparton, 3630
Tel: (058) 21 6352

Swan Hill Regional Art Gallery
Pioneer Settlement, Swan Hill, 3585
Tel: (050) 32 1403

University Gallery
University of Melbourne,
Cnr Grattin & Royal Parade, Parkville, 3052
Tel: (03) 344 5148

Victorian College of the Arts
Exhibitions Gallery, 234 St Kilda Road, Melbourne, 3004
Tel: (03) 616 9300

Warrnambool Art Gallery
214 Timor Street, Warrnambool, 3280
Tel: (055) 62 9920

WESTERN AUSTRALIA

Art Gallery of Western Australia
47 James Street, Perth, 6000
Contact Education Officer
Tel: (09) 328 7233

Albany Art Gallery
Town Council, Albany, 6330
Tel: (098) 41 5824

Bunbury Art Gallery
Princep Street, Bunbury, 6230
Tel: (097) 21 6173

Derby Art Gallery
Derby Cultural Centre, Derby, 6728
Tel: (091) 91 1443

Fremantle Arts Centre
1 Finnerty Street, Fremantle, 6160
Tel: (09) 335 8244

Undercroft Art Gallery
University of Western Australia, Nedlands,
6009
Tel: (09) 380 2006

Western Australia Institute of Technology
Heyman Street, South Bentley, 6102
Tel: (09) 350 7700